Jamie Lynn Spears

Biography

Growing Up in the Spotlight

Abraham H Garcia

Copyright © 2023
All rights reserved

The content of this book may not be reproduced, duplicated, or transmitted without the author's or publisher's express written permission. Under no circumstances will the publisher or author be held liable or legally responsible for any damages, reparation, or monetary loss caused by the information contained in this book, whether directly or indirectly.

Legal Notice:
This publication is copyrighted. It is strictly for personal use only. You may not change, distribute, sell, use, quote, or paraphrase any part of this book without the author's or publisher's permission.

Disclaimer Notice:
Please keep in mind that the information in this document is only for educational and entertainment purposes. Every effort has been made to present accurate, up-to-date, reliable, and comprehensive information. There are no express or implied warranties. Readers understand that the author is not providing legal, financial, medical, or professional advice. This book's content was compiled from a variety of sources. Please seek the advice of a licensed professional before attempting any of the techniques described in this book. By reading this document, the reader agrees that the author is not liable for any direct or indirect losses incurred as a result of using the information contained within this document, including, but not limited to, errors, omissions, or inaccuracies.

TABLE OF CONTENTS

1. The Business of Family

2. My Rising Star and All That

3. Teenage Angst

4. Never in the Shadows

5. Pregnancy and Perception

6. Breaking Up and Letting Go

7. A Butterfly Gets Her Wings

8. Much More Than the Right Guy

9. The Sacrifice for Stardom

10. The Day My World Stopped

11. A Good Mom

12. You Can Take the Girl Out of Louisiana

13. My Testimony

14. Breaking the Cycle

1.

The Business of Family

My story's beginning is well known. I was an oops, just like millions of infants around the world. My parents were already proud parents of Bryan, twelve, and Britney, nine, when I arrived. Money was hard for the family before I was born, and Daddy had turned to drinking-a lot and frequently. Momma owned and ran the Little Red School House, where she prioritised childcare over earnings. From what I can tell, these were hard times. Momma and Daddy had decided not to have any more children because they already had two healthy children and debts to pay. But then Momma awoke one morning feeling ill. She believed she was terribly ill at first, but after being examined, the doctor confirmed she was pregnant and about seven weeks along. "That can't be right. "My husband had a vasectomy," Momma said as she walked out of the doctor's office. Momma was furious when she returned home since Daddy hadn't gone for his post-op appointment. "Jamie, I thought you took precautions to prevent this from happening. I went around for days, convinced that I was seriously ill. And now I find out you never went to see for sure it took." Momma didn't speak to him for days, and she was enraged for weeks. Daddy acknowledged that another child would be joining the family. Momma simply needed some time to adjust to the notion of another baby at a time when Bryan and Britney were finally mature enough to care for themselves. My parents never contemplated having an abortion or placing me for adoption. They would figure out how to make it work. Bryan and Britney were overjoyed at the prospect of having a sibling, and everyone started making plans.

On April 4, 1991, I entered the world and forever altered the fabric of my family. I didn't make things simple for myself. Momma was forced to have an emergency C-section after hours of labour. I was a long and slender baby who quickly gained weight. We grew into a group of five, and from what I've heard, I brought love and brightness into everyone's lives. Momma's previous reservations about adding another child to her family vanished within hours of my arrival. I turned out to be a beautiful baby who brought her so much joy and filled a gap she had no idea existed. Because I was the youngest by nine years, I became everyone's baby, toy, duty, and joy. Bryan and Britney were overjoyed to get a new sibling. My siblings were involved in almost every area of my childhood. Bryan was a protective big brother who would feed and rock me on occasion. Britney became our mother's additional pair of hands, doing everything from bathing to feeding to playtime and diaper changing. Bryan and Britney both had busy lives, but they always found time for me. We were a close-knit yet complex family. I suppose we still are. My mother looked after me while my brothers and sisters went to school. I recall many meals at the table and many good times when I was younger. Everyone adored me and handed me around a lot. My parents say my theatrical side manifested itself early, since I spoke early and charmed my family with my babble. From toddlerhood on, I chatted about anything, made funny faces, and was generally entertaining. I had boundless energy and raced about singing and dancing. Momma describes me as intelligent, sweet-hearted, and strong-willed. Daddy came and went a lot. Momma was too preoccupied with the three children to be concerned about what he was doing. When he was present, he spent most of his time sitting in a chair, trying to persuade everyone else that he wasn't intoxicated.

Growing up in Louisiana, my recollections are filled with hot days in the sun and the craziness that comes with being part of a large family. Our family was tight-knit and full of affection. Every weekend, our backyard was packed with family and friends. A huge tree in the middle of the yard offered shade for the hours of playtime we all had. Momma cooked a lot of food when she could, and there was always a grill on. People would stop by throughout the day, as was customary in Louisiana. We spent several afternoons with neighbours and friends. We used to play outside, drive go-karts, and swim in our neighbour's pool. But I could tell there was something strange about my family from the start, with Daddy's troubles and the conflict between my parents. It would take several years for me to realise how different we were from other families.

Anyone who knew us before we became famous would tell you we lived in a modest house in Kentwood. Kentwood is a little community where everyone greets each other by name and asks, "How y'all doin'?"" It's the kind of environment where everyone knows everyone else's business and everyone is nosy. But don't cross a local because we look out for one another.

My favourite childhood memories are all of us sitting around a table together, eating Mommy's cuisine. RO*TEL chicken, peas and mashed potatoes, crabs-you name it, she made it. We all like her rural food, but boiling shrimp and crawfish with Daddy and Bryan was a family favourite. When someone asked whether there was any extra, she had to say no. Momma couldn't risk sharing what little food was available. Momma learnt to make do with what she had when money was short. She would feed my siblings and me first some nights. She'd then consume whatever we'd left behind.

I was the princess when I was younger. Bryan and Britney made me feel unique no matter what was going on in their lives, and they loved me despite my misbehaviour. Bryan visited my school and spoke with my kindergarten teacher one day. "How's she doing here?" he inquired."Jamie Lynn is one of our best and most well-behaved students," the teacher said, and Bryan laughed. "How about this one? No way. She never sits still!" It appeared early on that I knew who I was talking to.

We were your normal family, spending hours amusing ourselves with stupid challenges and outdoing each other in amusement. The celebrity and money came later, but not when I was younger. As a little girl, I never considered how much money we had or whether we had enough. My brothers and I did not suffer, but in retrospect, I can understand how the uncertainty in our lives led to financial troubles. We always had what we needed, but I knew better than to request anything costly. When Momma and her friend went shopping, I learnt that lesson early on. Momma's credit card was declined at Limited Too, so her friend had to pay for my things. Momma's anxiety belied her promises that everything was alright. I can still feel the sting of embarrassment to this day.

My father was well-known for starting enterprises and excelling at each task he took on. He did building and welding work. He also owned Granny's, a seafood restaurant famed for its crawfish and shrimp. He eventually donated it to Bryan, who eventually sold it. Daddy even opened the first gym in our neighbourhood, which was a huge success. My sister, I believe, also taught classes there. When big business arrived in Louisiana, the gym closed. He worked as a welder and boilermaker for many years. He did everything he could to assist the family in the best way he knew how.

The stress of providing for us sometimes led him astray. He had been in a loop of negative behaviour for years. Daddy never completely stopped drinking, but he did take pauses from time to time. The time between employment was the most difficult for him, and this is when he began drinking heavily. Family legend has it that he drank heavily. One of the more bizarre occurred before I was born. My entire family gathered to celebrate my great-grandmother Lexie's birthday at Pizza Hut. She was a huge fan of Pizza Hut. Momma worked all day but made an effort to dress herself and my siblings nicely for the occasion. The family waited for Daddy, who arrived swaggering in, inebriated. Momma was furious because he couldn't link phrases together and tried to slur, "I'm not drunk." Everyone took two steps away from Momma, sensing something was going to happen. "Get that ice chest down from there!" Momma ordered as

Uncle Austin was unloading the work vehicle." He positioned it in front of a tree and backed away carefully while Momma stomped around to the rear of the house, grabbed a shotgun, and blasted up that ice chest. The family just stood there watching her demolish the cooler. But Daddy insisted he wasn't inebriated.

Daddy believed that he was a good drinker and that no one could tell when he was drunk. But the strange part was that his entire demeanour gave him away. When his foot started tapping, you knew he was thirsty and was about to leave us for a time. Momma described it this way: "Sometimes things just get to be too much for him, and he takes off." As if that explanation made sense to a youngster. Momma attempted to shield him with excuses and keep us kids from seeing him drunk. And, as a small child, I had no idea how his actions affected everyone else. Something didn't feel right to me. Still, he was my daddy, and I desired his time and attention. He spent the majority of my life in that destructive loop. His drinking episodes usually brought me agony and misery. It would be many years before I could accept and resolve the seeds of bitterness sowed during this time-at Daddy for his drinking and at Momma for how she controlled her life.

Momma worked tirelessly to keep everything in order and to care for us. Britney's much older age made things a little easier to handle. She pitched in whenever Momma needed assistance. Britney took charge of cleaning and dressing me, and she dedicated herself to making me look great every time. Momma was grateful to have Britney and admits that my sister was much better at girly things than she was. I grew up thinking I had two mothers. Bryan would look after me when I needed it, and as Britney's career took off and Momma began to travel with her for work, his responsibilities increased. Daddy was occasionally present, but my relationship with him deteriorated as I grew older. It was difficult because I never knew which version of Daddy would come.

I was born with a huge personality and quickly learned how to catch people's attention. Everyone's reaction to my antics simply made me desire more attention, and I did everything I could to keep the spotlight on me. I would occasionally impersonate someone or sing a song. Our house was always filled with music. I used to enjoy watching and listening to my sister sing and make up dance routines. I wanted to join in whenever I could, and I tried to imitate my sister. My entire family enjoyed my wild behaviour. When I couldn't garner attention that way, I'd make trouble. I enjoyed hiding. It was a certain technique to get everyone's attention only on myself. I eventually emerged from concealment, and the range of reactions-relief, disbelief, and anger-made me laugh.

When Momma took us to a store, I decided to hide in the clothing racks. No one noticed me because I was so small. After a few minutes, I made myself known, and everyone breathed a sigh of relief. Momma made certain that someone was always keeping an eye on me from that day forward. I used to say the most absurd things at times. Momma held her breath several times, waiting to see what I would say in public. I liked making her cringe! But I made certain that Daddy was not around for my antics. That kind of action would not be tolerated by him.

Our family was undergoing a transformation by the time I started first grade. Bryan was a young adult contemplating his next move, while Britney was on her way to becoming a household celebrity.

My sister had a natural talent, with an affable demeanour and charm that secured her success in the entertainment sector. Britney worked hard to develop her talent, and at the age of fifteen, she already had an amazing résumé. Her music demo persuaded Jive Records executives to give her a shot. Momma and Daddy were overjoyed that their efforts were beginning to bear fruit. I, like my sister, took dancing and singing classes. My snark and dramatic personality immediately drew me to acting. Momma and Daddy made certain that I had the same opportunities to develop my skill as Britney. My sister was my inspiration. Britney wasn't simply talented; she exuded a comfort onstage that I wished I could replicate. I never wanted to be her career or follow in her footsteps; all I wanted was to capture her confidence and magnetism. Some have said that Britney's ability to perform inadvertently influenced my decision to pursue acting, but my propensity for portraying characters began at such an early age that it was more like acting chose me.

My sister's celebrity caused significant alterations in our family dynamics. Momma and Daddy recognized Britney's long-term success was a long shot, but they were going to do everything they could to get her in front of the right people, establish the right team, and compensate her appropriately. It was a strategy that worked because of the good fortune that came with Britney's hard work and talent. The familial dynamics evolved as bargains were struck. Britney had a dream, and her dream would have an impact on all of us. Although she was unfazed at first, my sister's life got more demanding as her fame developed. Everyone made sure her requirements were addressed, and we all took on the responsibility of assisting her as she advanced in her career. We have to keep her satisfied and working. I was so young when she first appeared on the world stage that I didn't see how things were changing. My parents always expected me to do what they said. That didn't appear strange in the parent-child connection at first. But I was raised to defer to Britney and act in ways that made things easier for her. Momma said things like, "Come on, Jamie Lynn, we don't want to upset your sister." It could be as simple as, "Let Britney do that first," or "If it's good for your sister, it's good for all of us." What complicated things even more was that Momma relished the attention that came with being Britney's mother. People were more interested in who she was than ever before, which I believe she enjoyed.

Daddy's few visits to the house never failed to perplex me. He was involved in whatever we did. Daddy emphasised on excellence in whatever we set out to accomplish. I believe Bryan struggled because he wasn't the star athlete his father desired. Momma maintained her strict parenting style throughout, but it seemed as if she had different expectations for my older siblings.

When we weren't on tour or running the business, we'd come home and just be a family. I like travelling on tour as long as I am accompanied by my family or a friend, but I prefer staying at home. Momma returned to the kitchen at home, and we were only kids. We all went to school for a few years. For us, life was perfectly normal. Things were better when Daddy wasn't drinking. We would occasionally shoot hoops or throw a ball around. He was my all-around armchair quarterback, offering advice and comments on everything. He and Momma had worked hard to launch my sister's career, and he was certain he knew just how I should go. That version of Daddy was tolerable even when we disagreed. The qualities I admired in him made the disappointment and rage that accompanied his neglect and absences all the more painful. I was frequently left to deal with these feelings on my own. My brother and sister, who were already teenagers at the time, had friends and freedoms that enabled them to flee.

Momma took it upon herself to teach Britney how to drive because she was a real educator. Momma took her out a few times before deciding it was safe enough for me to accompany her. My sister was fifteen at the time and didn't yet have her driver's licence. She was driving Momma's prized black four-door Lexus with a grey stripe. Momma adored that car, despite the fact that it had been a total loss. The automobile was often hot, but it was so much nicer than our prior vehicles. Britney was driving the Lexus down the road when it crossed the centerline. Another automobile entered our lane, and Momma had to grasp the steering wheel quickly to escape a crash. Back then, no one wore seat belts, and I was flopping around like a fish on land. Britney and Momma were yelling gibberish as the car rocked and careened into a ditch. "I'm fine!" we exclaimed one after the other." Momma quickly switched places with Britney. We all knew Daddy would freak out if he found out Britney was driving at the time of the accident. This was not the first time Momma tried to keep Daddy in the dark about everything. But Momma explained that she did it because she was concerned that an underage driver would exacerbate the insurance issues. All of our efforts to protect Daddy from losing his cool made me anxious. I was too young to comprehend their marriage's difficulties, yet I was wise beyond my years. Momma was always more concerned with Daddy's feelings than with doing the proper thing. In her own way, she was attempting to maintain stability and calm. Momma frequently put us in unpleasant situations rather than tackling them full on. We all pretended-said things or remained silent as Momma asked-to keep Daddy happy and their relationship maintained. It was easier to control Daddy on a "strictly need-to-know basis," allowing him to come and go as he pleased. The term "need to know" extended far beyond Daddy. As the family of a rising pop artist, we all had to learn how to manage information and secrets safely. Our family, like so many others, cared for, defended, and supported one another to the exclusion of all else-and sometimes even ourselves. Momma was influenced by circumstance, but Daddy's early traumas compelled him to embrace this mindset as a protective strategy. We defend one another at any costs.

Learning about my father's childhood helped me better understand him. Daddy's childhood was terrible. Paw-Paw June, my grandfather, was a physical man who utilised his hands to solve issues. In a tough situation, Maw-Maw Jean was a good woman. Women did not leave their husbands back then. Daddy's baby brother died when he was fourteen, and his mother died not long after. Paw-Paw June eventually married Maw-Maw Ruth, but Jean's mother, Great-Granny Lexie, also assisted in rearing Daddy. Despite the efforts of the women, my father was raised by an abusive father who placed unreasonable demands on his kid in all parts of his life. Daddy was forced to practise sports for hours on end, until he was exhausted. Paw-Paw June made Daddy shoot one hundred shots after practice for basketball. Daddy enjoyed basketball, but his father forced him to switch to the football field. He followed his father's advice and played collegiate football despite knowing he would have had a much bigger impact as a basketball player.

Momma's people were an entirely different breed. Momma's mother immigrated to America as a war bride and married a Louisianan. Her family was wealthy, cultured, and artistic. Music and art played an important role in her life. Momma makes no claims to musical ability, but I remember enjoying listening to her play the piano and sing in the church choir. My parents were high school sweethearts who remained together and grew closer. Momma's love for Daddy was a great force, but Daddy's was not. His affection ebbed and flowed throughout the years. Their diverse background and marriage resulted in a dynamic blend of passion, talent, and unwavering drive. We are the personification of their aims and hopes as their children, yet we are propelled by our own dreams and purpose. The upheaval in my parents' marriage took a back seat to the development and control of my sister's celebrity and my own career. Even after their divorce in 2002, they continued to collaborate and make decisions as a team. Daddy was still in and out of the house after the divorce. After all, family ties are complicated. For years, my family has had an incredible capacity to show up and eat together, even when we are at odds with one another. We managed to put our differences aside. The Spears family philosophy has always been, "When all is said and done, we are a family." We may not like or even love one another at the time, but it will pass, and we will find our way back. We've been doing it this way for decades. But as I grew older, the need to appear that everything was OK pushed me to put my own needs aside.

2.

My Rising Star and All That

Momma says she knew I was a natural-born performer the moment I started talking. I always had an audience since I had a large family and a lot of people around me. There's something about receiving a reaction from other people that I've always enjoyed. I'd bound into the room, whirling and swaying my hips. When I had someone's attention, I just let my imagination run wild and did whatever shenanigans came to mind. Everyone laughed at me because I was a baby. I, too, enjoyed singing, and as I grew older, I developed a variety of skits that showed all of my poor talents. I had aspired to be an actress by the time Britney's debut single was released. Momma and Daddy agreed to pay for vocal and dance training, as well as headshots and encouragement. The desire to be a performer was always mine, and I never felt as if my parents were living vicariously through me. I worked hard and enjoyed earning praise from everyone. Singing was only one aspect of performance that I enjoyed. My sister's voice was throaty and powerful, whereas mine was smooth and controlled. People felt we were unique, yet equally talented. But my primary passion was performing.

Britney's celebrity put a lot of hardship on her family. Britney's career carried her far from home, and she frequently travelled with Momma. Momma was clearly disturbed by Daddy's unreliability, and she worked herself to exhaustion just to keep everything afloat. Frustration resulted from periods of carelessness and contempt for Momma's needs. I believe my parents were so focused on keeping my sister's career on track that they neglected to pay attention to each other. Momma's rage and disappointment grew as the demands on her time grew. I was the only child who remained at home, but I wasn't the only one who noticed. We were all stressed. Britney eventually stated, "Momma, if you leave Daddy, I will buy you a house." That promise arrived just in time. Momma attempted to keep our way of life going for as long as she could. She was determined to keep her Southern habits in Louisiana, which included bringing friends and neighbours in and speaking with nice people. But Britney's celebrity changed everything. People began to drive past and walk around the property. Strangers approaching the residence became increasingly weird as time passed. Some people would approach the windows and peer inside, hoping to catch a glimpse of Britney's bedroom. It happened at all hours of the day and night. The feeling of protection was shattered one night when a man arrived in a white van just outside our door. "Momma," I cried, "there's someone parked outside and watching the house." We had no idea how long he had been out there or what his intentions were, but we weren't taking any chances. The scene seemed unsettling. Momma and I barricaded ourselves in the bathroom and dialled Rob, one of Britney's security guards, who stayed on the phone with us until the cops arrived. We soon moved into a new home that provided a more safe setting for me and Momma. We purchased two pedigreed German shepherds from Germany for increased security. We flew to California to meet the dogs, Roby and Ory, to make sure we were all on the same page. They were the best, most faithful dogs I've ever known, and I believe they would have killed to protect us.

Daddy didn't live with us in the new house, but he'd drop by anytime he pleased, and Momma just went about her business and let him in. It was one thing for Momma to leave Daddy. Staying away was a whole other thing. "Jamie Lynn," she'd claim to justify his visits. He's still your father." Their interaction compounded my own complicated sentiments for him. I couldn't rely on him to be the father I required. Seeing how my parents spoke one thing but did another weakened my capacity to trust them.

Perhaps my urge to abandon my pressures and travel to other places derives from my passion for playing characters. I felt altered whenever I quieted my mind to assume another persona. The liberating sensation only enhanced my enjoyment. I developed my talent by incorporating enjoyment into everything I made. The hours I spent creating characters let me see my future more clearly. I was always looking for opportunities to get in front of an audience. My practice grounds included school plays, church shows, and even neighbourhood auditions. I took any portions I could get my hands on. I portrayed one of Annie's orphans, appeared in several church musicals, and added singing to my dancing recitals. Because creative avenues were scarce in my little community, I was obliged to create my own. Momma was against me partaking in our school's beauty pageant, claiming she didn't want me to be a part of anything where females are assessed only on their appearance. I did some print advertising and a few commercial auditions. I directed national advertisements for Clorox and Pepsi. The dream demanded that I do anything that would allow me to express my creativity while also adding to my résumé.

Britney's entire family was immediately involved in the business of her profession. Bryan realised that hands-on learning was more effective than classroom education. He was brought under the wing of Britney's management team to master the fundamentals of dealmaking and people management. This led to the touring years, during which Britney's family accompanied her. It was the most effective way for us to remain close as a family. I was still quite young and loved it when we were all together. Despite the fact that I preferred being at home in Kentwood, touring with my sister gave an audience for my own performances. Momma always urged me to bring a friend on long-distance trips. We would spend our leisure time constructing mini-performances and personalities, filling the hours with hours of practice. The show's crew was vast, and everyone paid attention to me whenever I went into character or did an impersonation. "Jamie Lynn, you're a natural!" they exclaimed." I ran around backstage and hung out during the show's preparations."

It was inspiring to see Britney perform. I'd occasionally sit in the audience or watch from the sidelines. It astonished me how she managed to captivate the attention of thirty thousand people at once on a nightly basis. When she was finished, she always felt an adrenaline rush followed by tiredness. But her contented smile persisted. It was unnerving at times how exhausted she seemed after a show, especially as the tour entered its fourth or fifth month. I could see she was exhausted because of her hectic schedule, rehearsals, and performances.

The buses were loaded for the next stop after a full day of setup, staging, and performing. This was my opportunity to shine. With my sister's encouragement, and sometimes with the help of a friend, I would put on a mask and entertain everyone on the bus. Britney would make recommendations, and everyone would encourage me to do more. These one- and two-man acts served as the foundation for the characters I later introduced to television. These impromptu performances were occasionally filmed, and I enjoyed watching them again and over. Momma and Britney were so encouraging that I gained the confidence to dream larger.

Seeing my sister, Britney, own the stage taught me something about myself. I discovered I was more fascinated in the chameleon-like effect of transforming into someone else and developing a character that was so unlike myself. Still, getting an audience response, no matter how I did it, thrilled me, and I liked comedy. Having comedic timing is similar to having rhythm. After spending hours watching Drew Barrymore, Tina Fey, Jimmy Fallon, and just about everyone on Saturday Night Live, I desired to be a great comic performer.

For a few years, my life alternated between living in Kentwood and travelling on my sister's tours. When I returned to Louisiana, I resumed my normal kid life while continuing to concentrate on my acting and performing. I just kept going. Then I got fortunate. A Nickelodeon production assistant watched a film of me playing my characters in some behind-the-scenes footage from my sister's tour. Whatever she saw sparked a meeting with my team, and I was invited to audition for the Nickelodeon sketch comedy show All That. Sides, which were short sketches that I would play live in front of a team of producers, were emailed to me. This was before high-resolution movies and phone recordings were used to find talent. They also asked that I bring one of my own character sketches. I went with Louise McGillicutty, a character I made up while on tour with my sister. Louise, subsequently nicknamed Thelma Stump, was a cross between my great-grandmother Lexie and Rob, one of Britney's security guards.

I proceeded into the studios to an audition room, where numerous executives saw me and decided whether or not to hire me. I was frightened at first, but after I got into character, the pure joy of it took over. They'd throw lines at me, and I'd improvise in a way that emphasised my ability. I went home and waited for the call after they stated, "We'll be in touch soon." It took no more than a couple of days. One of the most exciting moments of my life was learning that I had been employed. I was overjoyed. This was the children's version of Saturday Night Live, a show that is largely responsible for my interest in sketch comedy. All That had been on hiatus for a little more than a year, and I was about to join a new cast.

I had only turned eleven when the contracts were signed and the cast was put together. All That had a lengthy summer shoot in Los Angeles. When we began filming, Mom and I flew out to California with my dog Izzy and slept in the Hollywood home Britney shared with Justin Timberlake. The neighbourhood had a terrific ambiance, but I was so busy working that I didn't have time to enjoy it. Time flies by when you're filming. As the sister of a newly minted pop icon, and with my own rising star, I needed to be cautious whenever I went out. Because of Britney's media presence, the paparazzi were always looking for a Spears story. I occasionally went out alone. But, as much as I enjoyed it, all of my friends back home were moving on with their lives and enjoying experiences that I wasn't a part of, and I felt confused at times. My attempts to display my talent were bearing fruit, yet a part of me ached to return home. With all of the travel and business, my inclination for staying at home, a tranquil location where I could unwind, remained. We'd travel back and forth between California and Louisiana as much as our schedule allowed. Unfortunately, the continual travel and demands on my time made caring for Izzy untenable, and I had to give her away. When I missed having my own dog, I would occasionally get to care for one of Britney's.

My shooting schedule for the show caused even more stress in our household. Britney and Bryan were preoccupied with their own projects, giving Momma the opportunity to visit me in California. I believe my parents formed a power struggle over the years, which grew as my sister, and later myself, became successful. Our journey into the entertainment industry propelled my parents into responsibilities that they had to learn on the job. There was no class or seminar series for Momma and Daddy as we became working artists. The pressures of our professions blurred the borders of parenting, and decisions had to be made for both my sister and me. Their relationship suffered as a result of this. In a matter of months, we moved from a simple Louisiana family to international fame. It became painfully clear that my parents' marriage was deteriorating, and there was nothing I could do about it. I knew things were bad between them, but at the very least I avoided the disgrace of their divorce. I was worried about the changes that a divorce would bring. I was more worried about how things would alter from day to day. I didn't want to divide weekends, forgo time with friends, or disrupt my life when I was younger. Momma felt moving would improve her relationship with Daddy and offer a more stable environment for us in our new house.

In the end, all of the drama and divorce were pointless. Britney's house gesture was for naught. Daddy still showed up whenever he wanted after we relocated, and Momma just let it happen. That was all for naught. Unfortunately, his drinking quickly took hold and eroded the fragile quality of our relationship. Over time, the idea that Daddy would continue to love me and be what I needed faded.

This was a trying time in my life. I grew to dislike the exact man I desired to adore. Years of longing for Dad to love me as I needed to be loved slowly led to disdain. I always wanted Dad to be a part of my life, but not knowing if he was drinking gave me a lot of concern. Much of my anxiousness was caused by Momma's failure to do what she should have done to protect me when he was on a bender. Daddy's actions and Momma's complicity robbed me crucial life experiences. We stopped talking, yet he would pop up in our California apartment or on set, much to my chagrin. He came to my basketball games during the months I resided in Kentwood. I couldn't trust what condition he was in, whether he was drinking or not. At times, I advised my mother not to tell Daddy about my games. Tormented, I repeatedly urged him not to attend my gatherings. The mere possibility of his appearance made me nervous. It was more than just the embarrassment his acts may have created; the fear interfered with my attention, and I was unable to develop the skill I thought I had.

The holidays were very stressful for my family. We'd all be together, but there was an underlying tension that everyone felt. Momma did everything she could to keep the unease at bay. She would spend hours cooking and trying to create a joyful environment in the house. We learnt to act as if everything was fine. Every Christmas ended up being the same. Daddy would leave when he felt he couldn't "deal with everything." It always tore me apart, and I knew I'd feel the sting of it for a long time. I remember telling myself, "I will not do this to my children." I had never had a pleasant Christmas until my first one with Maddie.

My work on All That saved my life. Although I enjoyed the regularity that daily life in Louisiana provided-school, activities, and friends-my employment required that I spend the summers in California filming. In many ways, performing was liberating because it allowed me to focus on anything other than my family's problems. Daddy ultimately sought assistance and entered a rehab in California as my brothers and I continued to work and produce. This helped me relax into my employment and enjoy my experience at the moment.

Every time I arrived to shoot a new season, I was filled with anticipation and excitement. But, as a moody adolescent, I also had spells of sorrow and a longing for home. I learned to hide my emotions and concentrate on my work. My brain was firmly ingrained with the Spears family trait of hiding emotions to get through the day.

Days on the set of All That were enjoyable, but the experience also served as a comedy master lesson. Surprisingly, when I first got on set, I felt shy, almost intimidated. The reality of appearing on a nationally televised event was sinking in. My only task for my first appearance was to run down a slide dressed as an elf and giggle. "Action," the director said, and I froze. It was impossible for me. Momma stopped offstage and gave me a look that said, "After all of your hard work to get here... now this?" But the cast was caring and supportive, and I was able to calm my fears and pull it off within minutes. Later, as we were filming the show's opening scene, the cast made me feel like a member of the team. I settled quickly and got my footing within a few weeks.

We were an ensemble cast, which reduced the amount of pressure I might have felt otherwise. My castmates and I were jointly responsible for the show's success. To be honest, it was the most enjoyable performance I've ever had. We'd make new characters every week and re-use ones that the crowd liked. I learned to push myself by playing characters who were unfamiliar to me. There was always a guest star cameo or a musical artist on the broadcast. Justin Timberlake, Nick Cannon, and even my sister made appearances. The musicians included nearly every prominent band or performer from the 1990s, including Destiny's Child, LL Cool J, Usher, the Spice Girls, and the Backstreet Boys. The cast and visitors would hang out in an extravagant greenroom that appeared on-screen for the audience. All That was a four-camera show, so we could rehearse Monday through Wednesday and film live on Thursday and Friday. The week would begin with a table read, during which writers would make notes and adjustments. Following the meeting, rehearsals would begin. When I wasn't rehearsing, I'd have costume fittings, hair and makeup sessions, and other activities to help shape the roles I'd be playing. We were all excited to get into costume and perform in front of a live audience by the time we started filming. On those days, the adrenaline was apparent. As a group, not everyone appears in every sketch. When we weren't on-screen, the cast hung around with the guest stars in the greenroom. We'd see everyone perform, meet the musicians, and have a good time.

The writers would construct characters and frequently solicit our feedback. I was occasionally requested to act out a written concept and apply my own spin to it. I loved it when the writers took a liking to one of my characters, like Thelma Stump, and put her into the program. Being a part of the process validated me and inspired me to create more personalities. "Thelma Stump," "Trashin' Fashion," and "Know Your Stars" were some of my favourite skits from the event. "Know Your Stars" was when one of the All That stars sat on a chair centre stage and a voice-over shared falsehoods about them. My favourite part was when I got snippy with the voice-over and upset him. Of course, I apologised, and he went back to telling ridiculous tales that no one would ever believe.

When All That was shot in the early 2000s, Nickelodeon had strict continuity requirements-no changes to our appearance were permitted. I lost one of my front teeth during a shoot. I couldn't have a tooth and a gap in the same photo. "We've got to get a flipper," someone added, referring to an attachable temporary tooth. I was back on set the next morning with my flipper in place, finishing the scene.

All That had a large following. Our show landed in SNICK House, Nickelodeon's Saturday night block designed to appeal to middle-aged to older teens. Former All That castmate Nick Cannon presented the block. I participated in On-Air Dare, Nickelodeon's version of Fear Factor, which aired during SNICK. All in the name of entertainment, I had to drink five gallons of blue cheese dressing, be drenched in eggs, and eat "earwax tacos." On-Air Dare has a fun fact: some of the substances used in the challenges are not what they appear to be. If you saw the blue cheese dressing challenge, you'll see that it was diluted for simpler intake. On set, the eggs were actually peaches. Slime, too, is composed of vanilla pudding and food colouring. Producers are required to safeguard the cast's safety by avoiding allergic foods and materials. To generate a wider audience, they would often have two stars from different programs compete against each other. Nickelodeon executives did an excellent job of incorporating their talents into various programs and introducing new faces. All That's producers were determined to broaden Nickelodeon and present artists from a diverse array of experiences and backgrounds. The sitcom won multiple honours, and several of the cast members went on to star in their own television shows. After a few seasons on the program, I began to feel more confident in my abilities as an actress and began to consider what might come next. Dan Schneider, the producer and writer of All That, saw my skill. He went on to create many other initiatives and was ultimately responsible for my opportunity to play a lead part in my next career.

3.

Teenage Angst

When my Nickelodeon contract began, I was overjoyed to be able to do what I loved, and I was appreciative, but being away from home so much left me sad. As much as I enjoyed being on television, I still enjoyed being at home and enjoying my normal tween life. Momma kept me humble, and the majority of the kids at home treated me the same way they always had-as Jamie Lynn. Others wanted to befriend me because of my celebrity, while others mocked me for it. Fortunately, my good pals remained faithful and continue to be so.

Contrary to popular belief, my tween years were rather quiet, save for being on a Nickelodeon show and having a pop star for a sister. When I returned to Kentwood, I reverted to being just like everyone else. I enjoyed sports, went to church organisations, and kept my tomboy attitude. Weekends were usually spent with friends, and whenever feasible, sleepovers were held at my house. My pals and I were constantly getting into mischief. When my friend Crystal and I were playing with a new video camera, I almost burned down the house. We decided to film one of our skits in the toilet, where my sister was lighting a candle. We were so preoccupied with what we were doing and the thrill of watching ourselves that we didn't realise we'd knocked over the candle. Minutes later, our laughter was cut short by someone yelling, "What's that smell?" Something is catching fire upstairs!" Crystal and I looked at each other, stunned. The fires were extinguished in minutes, and there was little damage.

My folks will tell you that I was a bright child. In some elements of my life, I was vocal and mature. Despite my sarcasm, I rarely felt comfortable communicating my worries and unhappiness about my family's changing relationships. I had two personalities: my public persona and my inner self. I was exposed to a wide range of experiences as a child, but when it came to males, I was innocent and honestly naive. I never played seven minutes in paradise or spun the bottle. Slow dances with boys were about as bad as I got when I was twelve. My partner and I would stand one foot apart, our hands softly placed just so. We'd sway gently and avoid making eye contact in whatever manner we could. By thirteen, I was allowed to go to a boy's house with my pals. I recall the first time a boy held my hand during a whole movie, and I thought it was a big deal. My first kiss came a few years later, when I was fourteen and dating a kid named Jarett Forman, who was a year older than me. He was such a nice person, and the experience was wonderful.

Being at home also presented me with new challenges. My family life was never consistent. My parents separated when I was ten, but for years before that, life in the Spears family was very dysfunctional. My father's long-standing practice of leaving for weeks at a time persisted, despite the anguish it caused, and my mother tolerated his actions. I was devastated by the consequences of his alcoholism and developed dread at the prospect of him showing up drunk to any of my sporting activities or performances. I was afraid of the embarrassment and shame that would ensue if he made a scene. My mother's permissiveness strained our connection and made life difficult for us. I couldn't understand how my mother could divorce him because of his irresponsible and inattentive behaviour and then rely on him to make sound decisions for me and my siblings. It just didn't feel right.

My parents were travelling for work or to help Britney for the majority of the time I was in Louisiana. My father was working, and Momma was on the road for weeks at a time with my sister. She always wanted me to go on tour, but I missed the routine of being at home. I'd spent many of my formative years on my sister's tour bus, and I didn't want to spend my vacations on one anymore. All I wanted was the rhythm of a quiet existence and the stability of family dinners. That, however, was not my experience. My brother,

Bryan, had moved to New York, and when my parents were gone, I spent extended periods of time with my friends and their families. Nobody ever made me feel uncomfortable, yet the longer I stayed, the more uneasy I grew. I always felt like I was imposing on people. The desire to return home became stronger with each passing day. My busy activity helped keep the grief at bay. I went to school, had lunch with my buddies, and then went home to study. I got involved in hobbies and sports to distract myself from the need to be at home at my own home. It developed a routine: I had a place and a routine in the spring and summer. I frequently found myself living a nomadic existence in the fall.

My experience with All That gave me the courage to explore moving on to something more serious. After three seasons on the show, I'd become a fan favourite, receiving praise for my performance and comedic timing. Nickelodeon approached me about creating a show in which I would play the starring role. Dan Schneider wants to create a show centred on me in addition to his work on All That. Zoey 101 was born after discussions and multiple brainstorming sessions. Dan thought I'd make an excellent Zoey. The premise of the show was to follow the antics of a young teen girl and her group of pals as they joined a new boarding school for girls. I was ecstatic. Although I enjoyed the camaraderie and daring aspect of All That, the chance to play a big role drew me in. Wow, I thought, my own program! That's incredible. Almost immediately, I began to consider how I wanted to portray this figure. Zoey might be anyone. How much of myself could Zoey contain? I hoped that by instilling some of my personality in Zoey, she would become someone females could relate to—a tomboy and quirky like myself, but brave in the face of boys and bullies. I had several meetings with the show's development team and producers to discuss Zoey. We held lunch meetings where we discussed information about the character and the backdrop for the program. Zoey's vision became clear, and seeing a part of myself in her made bringing her to life a breeze.

Nickelodeon arranged for a camera to film footage of me and a buddy attending the premiere in a New York City hotel as part of the Zoey promotional effort. After that, I never watched the show with anyone else, and I never watched it alone. All That's promotion was very different from Zoey's. For promotional ads and spots, the All That ensemble operated as a unit or in pairs. As the star of a new sitcom, I had my own publicist and stylist and was able to speak to the media and expose myself to the world. In a sense, I was propelling myself to the next level. I was both nervous and delighted to speak for myself and explore several things that were important to me. I recognized I had a voice and was concerned about how it would be heard. My sister and several contemporaries had appeared on The Ellen DeGeneres Show, Live! Regis and Kelly, TRL, and Good Morning America, and now I'm on them as well. I felt like I had arrived. Zoey 101 premiered on January 9, 2005, and it quickly became a smash. When it came time to return to the studio to begin filming the second season of Zoey 101, the cast and I were energised by our success. I liked how familiar the set was and how quickly the series was shot. The show drew some of the industry's top professionals. Dan Schneider, the founder and director, was exacting and insisted on professionalism. He knew how to obtain exactly what he needed from a rowdy group of teenagers who believed they were everything. It wasn't always easy to schedule and shoot scenes in a timely manner. Unlike All That, I was present for most of each episode. Every member of the crew was aware that time was a factor in every shot. Working with teenagers and youngsters was not the same as working with adults in the sector. I was only allowed to work roughly 10 hours a day according to union guidelines. Sometimes shoots would last longer than expected, and producers would have to devise a means to complete the scenes. We once shot an episode in which I appeared in every scene. We were aware that we were running out of time. A bucket was placed on my head as part of the screenplay so that all of the scenes could be shot. The bucket scenes could be done by a double, and I could finish the others.

Unfortunately, the show's stars' friendliness did not always translate into real life. Kristin Herrera, Alexa Nikolas, and I became fast friends during the first season of Zoey 101. Kristin, who played Dana Cruz, and I hit it off right away, but we all spent time together on and off set. We would have sleepovers on the weekends, go to the beach, the mall, or just hang around. We were just normal girls talking about fashion and boys. Alexa, who portrayed Nicole Bristow, spotted Kristin and I becoming closer, which caused some problems. Three is the worst number for girls since one is always left out. We had our fair share of fun and conflicts throughout the shooting season, just like any other girl our age. But gradually, I began to suspect that something was wrong. Rumours about me began to circulate among the actors and extras late in season one. It started with tiny lies, like people stating I was rude or bitchy. Everyone assumed Alexa was the one making the bogus statements. I approached the producers to express my worries. The rumours then took on a more menacing tone. I had the impression that a few people on set were trying to stir the pot and possibly provoke friction between me and Alexa. I was persuaded to believe that Alexa told extras that I stank and did other things over which I had no control. I'd leave the set ashamed and depressed. I cried several times after work and had to disguise my emotions. Concerns were aroused by the way her mother strode around the set as if she owned it and whispered to her daughter incessantly—apparently about me. Someone could have been feeding her misinformation that caused the troubles we were having. I began to assume that she wanted to have me fired from the show so that Alexa could be the star. I did everything I could to manage the situation, but it became increasingly difficult over time. I took my objections to the producers multiple times. Kristin departed the show after the first season because the producers desired a change, and she was replaced with Victoria Justice. The cast recognized that changes may be made at any time, and I wasn't getting any dirty stares or whispers. Things briefly improved. The introduction of a new cast member deflected Alexa's attention, but weeks later, another especially cruel rumour arose that I had lice. Some of the extras seemed offended, and I felt unjustified embarrassment.

I was an emotional wreck and in need of assistance as a result of the circumstance, so I sought advice from my big sister.

A few days later, a very pregnant Britney paid a visit to the set and spoke with Alexa. Britney requested that a PA bring Alexa to my trailer. I was working on set at the time. Alexa, who was obsessed with celebrity and connections, was overjoyed that my sister wanted to "speak" with her. When Alexa walked in, the door was open. Britney wasted no time in getting to the point. "Are you mocking my sister?" Spreading rumours and telling lies? That is not something you should do!" Britney told her that if she continued to treat others this way, she would lose her job. Alexa bolted from the trailer. Alexa didn't openly attack me after that conversation, and she was fired from the program after season two. She later revealed that she was bullied on the set of Zoey.

I took the high road and disregarded the story for years. I don't recall ever bullying someone, let alone a coworker on set. Given the way she handled me and attempted to turn the cast and crew against me, her statements appeared aimed to grab attention after her fame had faded. I couldn't change how she interpreted our interaction, but I can say I wouldn't intentionally injure her. That's just not my style. Based on all that had happened, and the fact that we were both thirteen, we both felt justified in our conduct. Looking back, I believe that all of them were typical childhood difficulties. However, in a professional atmosphere, with parents and producers present, the drama of these events was amplified. Some of it was due to simply spending too much time in each other's company.

I adored all of the boys on the show, as well as many other members of the cast. For me, the lads were far more enjoyable to be around at the time. Chris Massey, who played Michael Barret on the show, was a personal buddy with whom I am still in contact. Sean Flynn, Matt Underwood, and Austin Butler were a lot of fun to hang around with. Erin Sanders reminded me so much of her character, Quinn Pensky, that it was difficult not to like her. It felt like the entire ensemble shared a connection that didn't include me at points. Perhaps it was my own insecurities, but I believe they formed better bonds in California while I was home in Louisiana for the majority of the year. I was good in one-on-one situations. But when the whole gang got together, I felt a little on the outside looking in. Surprisingly, I was a little tense and shy at the moment.

I spent hours in the school trailer with our instructor, Ms. Patty, and my castmates while I wasn't shooting. School on set can be demanding at times. We needed to get things done faster than in ordinary school. Our classes were timed, and it's surprising how much you can get done in a small amount of time. We were expected to study and do tasks while appearing on one of the most popular television shows at the time. Some of my best recollections are of the cast just being kids and having fun. We all realised that schooling was necessary, but like all youngsters, we needed to let off some steam every now and then. We used everything available in the room to play jokes and pranks on each other. We'd do impressions and have amusing chats that got us way off subject. My favourite recollection is of us making bread as a class, as if we were in a Hollywood set home-ec class. But Ms. Patty was the very finest and got us to reach our requirements. We were our own strange and amazing family. Ms. Patty, the teacher I chose, was more than just a teacher. She also acted as a go-between for me and the producers. She was also in charge of our safety and making sure we weren't overworked. Ms. Patty enforced the established rules for entering and exiting, school hours, and rest. If there was a problem, she would act as a buffer or deal with matters that youngsters would find difficult to discuss. Ms. Patty stepped in when a parent was unavailable but the performer needed a voice. She was so patient and nice. Summer shots were much easier because there were no school pressures, but we still needed Ms. Patty for all the other things she did for us. She was always there for us.

The first two seasons of Zoey were shot throughout the summer at Pepperdine University in Malibu. Nickelodeon relocated the location to Valencia for the third season since we were planning to shoot twenty-six episodes instead of the usual thirteen, which would coincide with the start of Pepperdine's school year. It took some time for us to adjust to our new surroundings. The abandoned warehouses of an ancient military base replaced the coastal vista from the coast. Nickelodeon hired a team of engineers who entirely rebuilt old buildings and parking lots to match our Pepperdine residence. They recreated our dorm rooms and even designed our lounge area to make shooting scenarios easier. For the first time, we had additional staging areas, which made filming easier. I was astounded when I came onto the set and noticed the precise details they had replicated. Previously, we only had one camera on-site. We were now on a stage.

Momma and I leased an apartment five minutes away from the set. A normal day began with me getting out of bed, taking care of essentials, and getting ready for work. My days began early, generally in Mr. Michael's cosmetics chair. He kept my skin healthy with a morning ritual. When he was finished, one of the hairstylists gave me the Zoey look. Then I went to Ms. Khris in the wardrobe. Ms. Khris impressed me with her insight and vision. We'd talk about the episodes and the looks that worked for Zoey and me during the shoot week.

A parent or guardian was obliged by law to be on set with us at all times, save for brief periods of time when they might sign out for roughly ninety minutes. I was expected to act like an adult while being treated like a child. It was sometimes challenging to have so many people directing me what to do all the time.

I grew up beside Zoey. Playing Zoey didn't need me to transform into someone wholly different from myself. We were both strong-willed girls who were content with our lives. However, Zoey did not face the same real-life difficulties that I experienced, such as the weight of so much duty, homesickness, and the constant upheaval in my family. My parents' difficulties were not the only ones I was experiencing. Bryan was struggling to find his place in the world, while Britney was suffering from tiredness. Bryan was struggling to keep a job, and Britney was transforming right in front of my eyes. Britney would exhibit behaviours for weeks at a time, followed by moments of normalcy. Momma and Daddy would reassure her that she was fine and that she was just being Britney. But the nurturing and loving mother figure I respected, as well as the charming and adoring sister I admired, were morphing into someone I didn't know. I had to keep my cool while my family anxiously tried to help Britney. Many of the difficulties that afflicted my family were still too complex for me to comprehend. We were all going through significant changes in our lives.

Everything was perplexing to me, and I thought the only thing I could do was focus on my work and be the best professional I could be. I felt the strain of being the main character in a TV show, managing away from home, and remaining unwaveringly professional. I was strict with myself, keeping my weight low and not changing my appearance. None of this felt ridiculous to me since I was playing a figure who had to seem unaltered. But, although Zoey remained still on the screen, I was altering in real time. I transitioned from tween to teen and experienced all of the changes that came with it. When I was having a bad day, it was difficult to be the fun-loving Zoey. I went through the mood swings and physical changes that all adolescent females go through. When I was bloated from my upcoming period, I often struggled on shoot days. I'd collaborate with Ms. Khris to select clothing that would blend seamlessly from one scene to the next. I thought I was five pounds heavier just days before my period, yet I miraculously dropped the weight within hours of my flow beginning. Ms. Khris and the wardrobe staff were courteous, and I appreciated their assistance. Mr. Michael turned out to be much more than just my makeup artist. He resembled a guardian angel. My teen skin was prone to breakouts, and he instilled in me the value of proper skin care. He cleansed my face with hot towels perfumed with mint and eucalyptus and helped me rest after a busy day. He made me feel better about myself by validating my feelings. Mr. Michael was gifted and worked his magic to make me seem youthful and zit-free. Most significantly, he noticed when I was in distress. He would move at half speed to slow down my morning and give me the time I needed to clear my mind. Mr. Michael would be held accountable if this caused a delay in the schedule.

Momma and I resided in numerous residences across the Los Angeles area throughout the series. We relocated from Santa Monica to Marina del Rey, and then to Valencia, to be closer to the show's new venue. We explored moving in with my sister in Malibu in order to create a more united family environment and to support Britney, who was going through a rough patch. As much as we all wanted to be together, it became clear that something was wrong in Britney's world. I initially assumed it was the aftermath of her divorce and the media's preoccupation with her. My generally pleasant and free-spirited sister, on the other hand, continued to evolve into someone else—someone who was disturbed and paranoid at times. She would occasionally lash out or disregard me for no apparent reason. Britney would always feel guilty and apologise later. As far as I could tell, her chaotic life lacked any type of organisation or schedule. Momma could tell Britney needed help, but she insisted she was alright.

Momma was torn between providing a secure haven for me and remaining close to Britney during this trying time. Finally, we made the only logical decision and moved into an apartment near the set, giving it a homey atmosphere. Momma did everything she could to look after my sister. Someone on our set gave me another dog. Dogs offered me unconditional love and attention, which brought comfort and served as a reminder of home. Ally, a Yorkie poo, was by far the worst-behaving dog I'd ever had. She was a terror, fleeing and wreaking mayhem. Because of my demanding schedule, I didn't have time to provide Ally with the training and care she required. I eventually had to give her up as well.

Momma and I were beset by the regular mother-teen daughter issues. We would lash out at each other, and when I was very irritated, I would push her buttons. Everything came to a climax one day when she became emotionally stretched and snapped. She was upset and yelling at me, but when that didn't work, she began striking me with a huge beaded purse that contained, among other things, a camera. She swung the bag around and landed five hits on my shoulders before stopping. I hurried out of the apartment and to the shopping mall close to where we lived. I called my brother from a pay phone. "Bryan, Momma's insane." She refused to allow me to phone you or Britney.``

The next day, I arrived on site to film the Halloween episode in which I would dress up as Marilyn Monroe. Mr. Michael spotted some scratches on my neck and shoulder area as I was doing cosmetics. With concern in his eyes, he glanced at me. "What happened here, Jamie Lynn?" he inquired." I shook my head and began to cry." We didn't talk, but he gave me the space I needed to process my feelings. I eventually shoved all of my emotions down and went to work, as planned.

I missed home more than ever. My friends and boyfriend, Casper, were having adventures in Louisiana that I felt I was losing out on.

And Casper was greatly missed. I met him at a church youth group event a year and a half ago. Who can resist a handsome boy in a Dodge truck with a hog in the back? Yes, a full-grown pig. He was different from the other boys I knew at the time, and he went to a rival school. He was simply a handsome young man, and I was smitten with him. I loved having him to myself. We began quietly enough, texting and conversing. For a while, that was all there was to it. Momma never let me stay out late or spend time alone with any boy. However, teenagers usually find a way. Casper was cunning from the start. He gradually lured me into feeling at ease with the physical aspect of our relationship. I knew very little about sex and everything that went with it, including birth control. I mistook the rhythm method for a band from the 1970s. I just let him handle it. He'd sometimes pick me up in town and drive till we could park alone. Other times, when he knew no one else would be present, we went to his house. It was more exciting because we were sneaking around. Our affections for one other grew stronger.

The distance brought with it an idealisation of him and our relationship. Our honeymoon period had passed, and I was free to reminisce about our time together and fantasise about more romantic days ahead. I was falling in love for the first time and didn't know how to deal with the fact that we were over 1800 miles apart. I was grumpy and resentful at times. Momma's life was less demanding than mine. Bryan had moved to California with his wife and children, and Britney was already a mother of two sons, one year apart. Momma had all of her children and grandchildren in California, and she had plenty of time to spend with them. She could even call on Daddy when she needed him. Daddy and I had stopped talking at this point. I didn't want him anywhere near us, and Momma letting him in the apartment felt like a betrayal. When he came over, I locked myself in my room if I was at home. She was aware of my feelings, and as a result, my animosity intensified. It became harder to maintain our cordial friendship as the dynamics between my adolescent self and Momma shifted. Momma walked a fine line in order to please everyone. She failed to recognize that no one person can be everything to everyone. Someone is always sacrificed. Momma would flee whenever there was a rumour of a conflict in Malibu.

Even when things went wrong, Momma always wanted everyone to believe everything was fine. Not only were professional appearances important, but so were personal ones. She was a terrific pretender, but no matter how convincing she felt she was, everyone, including me, saw through the gaps. I was filled with a traitorous and fierce resentment.

I was expected to do my tasks at home after a hard day of shooting and school. My adolescent brain despised her for it. She wasn't doing anything. How come I have to handle everything while I was the only one with a full-time job? I ignored my obligations and refused to tidy up after myself or clean because I was exhausted. There was dirty clothing strewn over the floor, and clean garments were rarely found in drawers. I occasionally forgot to walk my dog Ally, and she left a mess inside. My room had turned into a pigsty. I was a stressed-out teen who worked on set for ten to twelve hours a day. Most days, I thought of my job as a hard-won prize. But there were occasions when I got enraged and aggressive. Except for a few instances when I was brusque or distracted on set, I was mostly professional. Regardless, I always arrived on stage prepared. I would be punctual and know my lines. I saved my frustration for after work. Fortunately, I wasn't the only depressed adolescent onset.

Aside from the juvenile angst, we had shootings that were difficult on their own. On one shoot, we were in the scorching California sun, which is notorious for turning grapes into raisins. We were shooting on a blacktop parking lot in temperatures well into the hundreds. Tents and portable air conditioners were erected, but it didn't help the workers and extras who were rushing around. People began to faint, and ammonia cloths were kept on hand to resuscitate them. Even on difficult days, we all felt a tremendous feeling of pride just for being a part of the program.

I'd spent the most of my adolescence on Zoey, and my contract was nearing an end. After four seasons, Zoey had developed to the point where I felt it was time to terminate the show, and I honestly felt like I had outgrown her. I never discussed continuing Zoey in any way with Nickelodeon. I was eager to go on to other assignments that would allow me to grow as an actor. Nickelodeon concurred. Zoey 101 gave me a tremendous education on what I needed to be good at in order to make a show succeed, as well as all of the components that go into making a show successful. It still amazes me how all of the elements-production, crew, hair and makeup, and filming-have to come together under such tight time limitations. Everyone had to work in unison.

Receiving praises and honours for our work as performers was not only rewarding, but nearly assured that we would find new positions. Everyone was filled with mixed feelings as we shot the final episodes of Zoey 101. We'd spent years together, and we were proud of the work that had helped Zoey 101 become one of Nickelodeon's most popular shows. With so many honours and the show's popularity, we all thought we'd be able to find new chances. The anticipation was intense. But there was a sadness about the end of the concert that even we teenagers could understand. The consistency of the labour had provided everyone with stability and cash; the friendship made the days more enjoyable. The success of the show had executives salivating. Other studios, production businesses, and music labels, in addition to the network, contacted me. But I didn't want to just dive right in. I was thinking about what would happen next.

I spoke with music producers and other production professionals throughout the Zoey process, but I never felt like they were interested in my professional goals. They knew that as long as I was willing to be sculpted and moulded to their liking, I was a bankable commodity. Executives weren't interested in me; they were interested in Jamie Lynn Spears' brand. They intended to turn me into a commodity that they could influence and sell. I had been playing the same character for several years. My love was acting. For the first time in my career, I would be able to select a position or project that spoke to me on a deeper level. The thought of using my free will seemed liberated. My plan included a shift to movies and music, whilst other members of the ensemble intended to stay in television. Victoria Justice was to star in her own sitcom, Victorious. Everyone else involved with Zoey 101 intended to go on to new ventures in the industry as well.

Fans fell in love with Zoey, and her popularity has remained strong for almost ten years. Apart from my peers, who frequently enthuse about Zoey 101, there are hordes of new Zoey 101 fans who discover the reruns on Nickelodeon or online. I love that the series has been loved by numerous generations of families. Surprisingly, my older daughter, Maddie, seems uninterested in watching me on film, and my younger daughter, Ivey, is too young to watch. I am frequently asked about a Zoey 101 reunion or a remake of the show, whether in person or on social media. Zoey has such a strong connection with her followers that they feel compelled to know how she turns out as an adult. I'm working hard to bring Zoey back to the screen.

The show also afforded me the opportunity to perform its theme song, "Follow Me," which my sister co-wrote. A current version of the song was recently produced and recorded by me. To appease the fans, I requested many of my original castmates to film a video for the song's remake. It was difficult since we executed a one-day shot that was hindered by COVID-19 protocols. That day's shooting schedule was ridiculous, with temperature checks and sanitation regulations. The years apart faded once we were all again in the same room together. We arrived as grownups, yet the performance transported us back to 2004. With the release of the song and video, new suspicions regarding a Zoey 101 reunion show surfaced. I'm looking forward to working on another Zoey 101 project, whether it's a feature film or a television series. The cast is excited to rejoin and bring the characters up to date. We've been talking about reinventing the series. Some intriguing ideas have been presented by producers and authors. Hopefully, a modernised version will be released shortly.

4.

Never in the Shadows

Growing up as the youngest Spears child was one of the best parts of my life because I had everyone's love and attention. Both of my siblings made sure I was included, nurtured, and treasured from the day I was born into the Spears family. Never in my life did I feel like I was competing with any of them. Britney always put me front and centre, shining the spotlight on me.

My status in the family was unique because I was a baby for more than nine years. When I came, my brother was a teenager, and Britney was already pursuing her career. Momma worked at the school, while Daddy had a variety of jobs. When they weren't working, they were all about Bryan and Britney's interests. Momma helped Britney by arranging for whatever lessons they could afford, transporting her to auditions and shows, and getting her in front of an audience. Daddy had a very different approach to his children's interests. As the son of an abusive perfectionist, Daddy picked up some of the strict traits that come with that type of upbringing. Daddy was never physically abusive, but his unwavering perfectionism embedded itself in all of us. The family credo had already been instilled in the synapses of my brain by the time I intellectually grasped it. If you're going to accomplish something, you should be the best at it. We couldn't do anything half-assed. That was a difficult level for Bryan to reach. He was a good athlete and a good student. But his performance fell short of Daddy's expectations, and Bryan battled with failing him at times. Bryan was merely my big brother, and I cherished him. Despite our age difference, he was always interested in me. As the bigger brother, he would watch after me and celebrate my accomplishments. He never seemed bothered by my presence and seemed to enjoy my immature character. If I sassed him, he sassed me back. He'd take me out, typically with one of his girlfriends—and Bryan was never without a girlfriend. Everything changed when I started stringing sentences together. He rapidly realised that I was the boss.

Momma and Daddy decided to go away for the night one time. Momma was hesitant to trust Bryan on his own, but his buddy Jennifer was scheduled to spend the night with us. Britney was visiting our cousin Laura Lynn. It didn't take long for anarchy to break out. By the time it came time for bed, I was in my room, attempting to sleep, and he had a backyard full of teammates and girlfriends. I was able to hear everything. Someone knocked on my door, and I swear he had facial hair. The sounds persisted, and I decided to investigate. Kids were drinking and listening to music. None of this troubled me until I noticed my kiddie pool was full of beer cans. That truly irritated me. "Oh mister, you're in real trouble," I said as I approached Bryan. I'm gonna tell Momma all about this." He turned me around and told me to go back to bed. My sister came in the next morning, stating she had heard what was going on. Bryan assigned Britney to clean-up duty. Momma called to see how I was doing. Britney's evasiveness alerted her to the fact that something was awry. "Momma, Bryan had a bunch of friends here," I stated as I demanded the phone. I slept with a man with a beard and there was beer in my pool!"

Britney and I have a sisterly closeness because of her love for me as a child. Being Britney Spears' baby sister is nothing like what people think. Britney's from the moment I arrived. Momma was frequently working and caring for the family. She also had to deal with the complications of an addict husband. Britney became like a second mother to me. She was much older than I was, and she relished the position of caregiver. My mother was nice, but my sister treated me as if I were her own American Girl doll. She used to spend hours playing with me when I was a baby. She would dress me up and make me seem lovely. Momma used to do my hair, but she soon discovered that Britney was far superior. Britney would get up early to see me before going to school. Our friendship evolved alongside us. Britney noticed how theatrical I was and encouraged my early shenanigans, which is how I learned to perform in front of others. And I was in pain. Britney would sing at regional gatherings, and I would stand onstage and bow as she finished her song. My sister thought it was cute. When I think back on some of the things I did, I cringe.

Momma was forced to bring me along when my sister joined the Mickey Mouse Club when I was a toddler. That troupe of entertainers was a lot of fun to be around. I was everyone's little sister, and my shenanigans drove them all insane. One afternoon, we were relaxing on the grounds of the hotel where we were staying. I ran away from Momma, and the Mouseketeers were all racing about hunting for me. They had no idea I was only moving around a single tree trunk to be out of sight. The hotel was surrounded by a vast body of water. Momma was in tears, worried that I had fallen into the water. When the youngsters discovered me, they laughed. I just giggled and said, "Gotcha!" Britney didn't chastise me. She hugged me and whispered, "You little devil." Another time, Momma was driving a few of us from the set, and JC Chasez's dad walked up to Momma's window and spoke with her. My quick-thinking mind took over. I leaned past Momma out the window and said, "I already have a daddy!" Everyone laughed and I don't think anything like that ever happened again. Being on the Mickey Mouse Club set with those incredible young performers taught me early on that actors, even the most famous ones, were just people. We were truly like a huge family, and I still think of them fondly. Christina Aguilera, JC Chasez, Ryan Gosling, Keri Russell, and Justin Timberlake, who was my sister's boyfriend on and off for many years, were among the cast members.

Simply said, I adored Justin. He was more than just my sister's boyfriend. Justin was my first example of a generous and caring young man. For a long period, he and my sister were happy together. Momma and I used to hang out at Justin's family's place. We went swimming and had cookouts. Justin was always kind to me, and his relationship with Britney was the only one in my life that provided me with stability. That may seem unusual given how it ended, but they adored each other and made me a part of their relationship in the nicest manner possible. Justin treated me like a little sister and lavished attention on me whenever he could. I have so many memories of Britney, Justin, and me together—many of them on vehicle excursions to various locations. I was never an inconvenience to either of them. He gave me a video camera for Christmas one year. My sister will undoubtedly object to my recollection, but I know that gift was entirely Justin's idea. He knew I like doing skits and felt the camera would provide me with another creative outlet. Britney's willingness to make me the third wheel in her relationship was appreciated, and I will be eternally grateful for the memories they provided.

Unfortunately, their divorce had a significant impact on me. Their consistency was the best example of a loving marriage I had ever witnessed. When it ended, I was completely heartbroken, and I believed it was a catastrophic loss in Britney's life as well.

I watched as my sister, Britney Spears, rose to fame as a music singer, and then as a one-named icon, Britney. Life changed on a daily basis for her, but for many years, not much changed in terms of her role in my life. She adored me as a baby and continued to do so as I learned to sing and perform my own skits. My sister lavished me with love, attention, and praise far into my adolescence. She, like Momma, was one of my strongest supporters, telling me that I was talented and would make an excellent performer. To show her support, my sister continued to make me the tour bus's night star and gave me a stage to perform for the crew. I spent months on her numerous tours, and those experiences boosted my confidence. My skits are legendary—at least among those who have spent time on tour buses. But my sister was more than just a cheerleader for me.

Britney was only irritated with me a few times. In our backyard, she had built a modest child-sized playhouse. The playhouse resembled a house, complete with a kitchen and living room. I used to run around as a kid, catching frogs and insects. I began collecting species, storing them in the playhouse, and constructing my own animal farm. I had nearly demolished Britney's playhouse by the time she returned from a summer stint in New York. She wasn't thrilled with me at the time, and she let me know. But Britney, who was prone to holding grudges against others, quickly forgave me.

Aside from her love and support, Britney was a wonderful sister. That isn't just me paying respects to a living legend. She was good at keeping her persona out of our sisterhood for many years. The rest of it-stardom, talent, and a tumultuous media shitstorm-has nothing to do with the sister I adore. The only reason I bring up tabloid gossip is to point out that so much of what has been written about her is a diluted version of the truth. I'm not here to debunk the myths about my family; I just want to share my experiences and the complicated blessings that come with being a member of the Spears family. The paparazzi were invading Britney's personal space and private life long before articles and reports about her dominated news outlets. I saw her endure the bullying and offensive verbal attacks, as well as the photographers who followed her around whenever she was in public. To be honest, the paparazzi would often intrude on private moments as well. One such incident occurred when Momma and Britney took me and a friend to the local pet store. By the time we were ready to leave the shop, a swarm of people and photographers surrounded the storefront and our car. I was hunched in the back car with my pal in shock. As Momma tried to move the car forward slowly, she and Britney were yelling in vain to get people to move out of the way. A man started screaming that she had run over his foot. Momma was shouting that it wasn't true. He told his wife to call 911. Once the police arrived, Momma insisted that the man was lying and demanded that an officer go with the couple to the hospital to make sure he didn't try to inflict damage on himself. She was worried he'd hit himself with a hammer or something. It was complete pandemonium. As it turned out, the man was evaluated by the local hospital and hadn't suffered any injuries. But this kind of reaction was a regular occurrence anytime my sister tried to go out in public. I wasn't quite a household name yet, but if we went anywhere together, cameras and lights went off at fantastical speeds.

Some people feel the paparazzi have the right to photograph a public figure no matter the circumstances. But what most people don't truly understand is that fame doesn't dehumanise you-it actually forces you to respect and appreciate your privacy. With the help of California lawmakers, and after multiple dramatic incidents, politicians realised legislation needed to be enacted to protect people from the paparazzi. In 2009, a law was passed that is sometimes referred to as "the Britney Law." I was happy when I learned there would be protections in place for both famous and private citizens.

As I mentioned, the recorded skit sessions on my sister's tour bus are what led to me catching the eye of a Nickelodeon producer. Britney believed I could accomplish anything, and she made sure to tell me and everyone else. It never occurred to me I could possibly fail. That didn't even register in my head. I was privy to watching and sharing in my sister's journey to success, and honestly, I thought, If she can do it, so can I. Momma made us believe that anything was possible if we dedicated ourselves to it; Daddy taught us that if you are going to do it, you must be the best. With those tenets reinforced year after year, and watching Britney's rise to fame, how could I feel any other way? It was never if, but how was I going to get there?

My path to fulfilling my dreams was paved the moment Nickelodeon expressed interest. There's no disputing that Britney's celebrity helped me. But once inside, I had to demonstrate my talent and work ethic. Studios constantly hire new actors and retain those who continue to perform. Every day, I had to prove myself. Nothing was given to me. My sister was overjoyed when she found out I'd been recruited for All That. She realised that a kids' variety show may lead to bigger things. Despite her booming career, Britney always made time for me and supported my show by making appearances on a regular basis. I enjoyed having her on set, and her visits allowed us to catch up. It also didn't impact the ratings.

Momma and I were living at the house off Sunset Boulevard where Britney and Justin lived, as I previously stated. I was filming just a few miles away when they were busy performing. We would hang out as sisters when she wasn't on tour and I had a few hours off. Despite our age difference, our life experiences brought us closer together. The days were spent in the water, creating up dances and acting out impromptu performances. My sister once choreographed a routine to P!nk's "Get the Party Started" for me. Britney directed the entire affair, which we shot with my video camera. She videotaped me in our elaborate homemade movie after hours of honing the motions. I was singing to the camera, being my snarky self, and pretending to be a celebrity. My sister was usually making me feel cool. We sometimes spent the entire afternoon examining her land. Britney had lemon trees that grew more than just lemons, I swear. In truth, there were most likely a few different fruit trees planted among the lemons. We'd go fruit picking and running around the hills. I was still a child, and Britney was still a child at heart. We spent our days in Louisiana constructing forts. She'd drive me and my pals into town, and we'd load up the car with supplies like wood, tape, and tarps. We spent hours making our own private worlds and enjoying the outdoors, and it allowed all of us to be kids again. I believe that being with me, just playing, allowed Britney to reconnect with a part of her life that she had missed.

My early years in Hollywood were enhanced by having my sister as a constant companion. But by the time I was twelve and learning about the darker side of celebrity, my sister's problems with her own life and the media had become more intense.

My family celebrated Christmas in Kentwood in December 2003. My sister bought a new Mercedes for Momma as a surprise. Britney and Bryan stole the car on Christmas Eve and went out to celebrate. Britney wanted to party her way through the agony of her separation with Justin. They ran across an old friend from town, Jason Alexander. Jason and Britney grew up together but attended different schools. According to legend, when Jason was a child at daycare, he bullied a classmate. Britney, four, stepped in and beat him up. Jason rose to prominence in our small community. He was frequently up to no good, and everyone knew he was trouble. But Britney was unconcerned about any of that. She and Bryan didn't show up until the next morning, looking as if they had been awake all night. The interior of the car was a shambles. The rear seat was cluttered with debris, bottles, and even a razor blade. Momma was terrified and refused to get in the car. But it was Christmas, and we were all going to have a good time.

Nonetheless, my sister's generosity was limitless. Britney organised a girls' trip to Nevis in the Caribbean. Sandra, our aunt, had been fighting cancer, and we were all looking forward to the vacation. Momma, Aunt Sandra, Britney, Laura Lynn, me, and a handful of pals flew to Nevis the day after Christmas. I saw Britney was being secretive and keeping her distance right away. She smoked heavily and drank a lot of cocktails. My sister, who was still like a mother to me and was usually well-dressed, began to disintegrate even in the way she presented herself. It felt strange to see her dishevelled. We were getting ready for supper when I suggested a nice dress like the one Laura Lynn was wearing. "You want me to dress like a grandmother?" mocked Britney. Huh?" It was the first time she had snapped at me in such a contemptuous manner. She refused to spend time with her long standing closest friend, Laura Lynn, and instead left us to do our own thing. She preferred not to be with us. I was really hurt by her rejection. My sister was moving on without me after years of making me a priority and spending time with me. I imagined myself as Woody from Toy Story. I was her favourite until she replaced me with her version of Buzz Lightyear. Her apathy was difficult for me to comprehend.

Britney has no plans to slow down. That week, the festivities continued. On New Year's Eve, we returned to Hammond's private airport, and as everyone save Britney and Laura Lynn disembarked, Jason and a handful of their pals boarded to fly to Las Vegas for the holiday. I had a feeling this was a poor idea. Something was very wrong with her. "Now don't go and marry Jason while you're there, Britney!" was the last thing I said before she departed. She rolled her eyes at me and mumbled something akin to "as if." But, within hours, we learned that she had married him in a haze of substance. My parents flew to Vegas to try to mitigate the tragedy. I was left behind, having to cope with everyone's gossip and talk from all over town. I hid my discomfort and humiliation by downplaying the entire incident and pretending it was exaggerated. Inside, I was terrified and unsure of how to go. I was feeling abandoned.

The marriage dissolved within hours, but my sister's life was only getting started. Jason continues to try to make himself relevant in Britney's life by saying gibberish. He even offers interviews about our family in order to generate interest in himself.

My sister returned to Louisiana, and my family handled damage management while attempting to limit public consequences. Everyone was more concerned with my sister's emotional state than with public image. Britney's behaviour remained inconsistent, and all I desired was her interest and acceptance. I wished to reclaim my sister. Instead, I noticed the extent of her difficulty. She was unstable and paranoid. She once remarked to me, "Baby, I'm scared," and then took a large knife from the kitchen, dragged me to my room, and locked us both inside. She slid the knife into the drawer of her bedside table and simply said, "I'm scared." She required that I sleep with her. Britney was packing her belongings and returning to her home in Los Angeles just a few days after this episode aired. I knew something was wrong, but I couldn't do anything about it. Everyone was too invested and refused to do what needed to be done. Something was off, and I felt uneasy when she departed.

Bryan's life was just as hectic, but he didn't have the celebrity. He was still battling with work and occasionally worked for both me and Britney. He also had other occupations along the road. He lived in New York for a while, and I enjoyed visiting him there. We established a regimen that took us to our favourite places, such as the Times Square eatery Mars 2112 and FAO Schwarz. Bryan was a womaniser who drew women to him like bees to honey. He soon began dating my manager, Graciela, and they got married. However, his problems with job and money management persisted.

But, for the most part, I was an egocentric tween who was able to compartmentalise and keep all the family drama out of my mind. I was preoccupied with being myself—the tween television star and the Southern tomboy who adored her home.

I felt confident in the direction of my career after signing up for Zoey 101. Britney was more balanced at the moment, and I was relieved that she was doing well. She'd found love with Kevin Federline, married, and given birth to two lovely boys. Her emotional changes, which I referred to as episodes, were carefully controlled, and no one ever found out about her difficulties. My family thought it was best for everyone. I agreed because I was trained to support my family in all circumstances.

Britney made a home near where I was shooting, so we could hang together whenever our schedules allowed. As more people became aware of the event, my name began to appear in periodicals and online reports. Photographers took shots of me, and I began to understand how my sister's daily violation felt. The amount of paparazzi multiplied whenever we went anyplace together. It was completely ridiculous. I despised attention and would do anything to avoid it. There wasn't much free time to go out during my shooting schedule, and even when I got older, I didn't want to go to Hollywood parties. I was affected in some ways by seeing the bad impact of so much attention on my sister, and I'd dealt with some of the animosity she faced myself.

Britney was changing yet again, despite my love for her. She began to go through a very trying period. My fun-loving, sweet-natured sibling had softened. This time, I blamed her problems on her divorce and having two infants in the same year. Even though we were only three feet apart, she grew aloof once more. She was moody, and her irregular conduct bothered me. At the start of Zoey, she would come over on occasion to hang out on set. Everyone, especially me, enjoyed having her there. The sister I knew had vanished by the end of the third season, when Sam Lutfi had penetrated her life. She arrived at a Zoey shoot in a bad mood. Britney, the kind girl, had vanished. In her place was an irate woman who was mad enough at Momma to yell at her in public. It was the first time she had ever made me feel humiliated. For a while, Momma and I just made excuses for her behaviour. Sam, a man who weaselled his way into Britney's life with great stories and bogus promises, was isolating her from the wonderful people in her life.

Sam Lutfi sought to entice Momma into a jewellery scheme months before he became Britney's self-proclaimed gatekeeper, marketing stones on HSN. Jackie Butcher, Paul Butcher's mother, introduced Momma to him. On Zoey 101, Paul portrayed Dustin, my younger brother. Momma and I met Sam at the Grove, a shopping and dining centre in Los Angeles. I knew he was bad news the moment I met him. "He's creepy," I told Momma, "and makes my skin crawl." I didn't want him in our midst. She met with him again and turned down his proposition. He didn't say anything for a while. Weeks later, my sister was at a nightclub when Sam approached her, claiming to be a friend of Momma's. We weren't sure if he orchestrated the introduction or if they just happened to be at the same club. Sam gradually worked his way into her life. He defrauded Alli Sims, a family acquaintance who worked as Britney's assistant at the time. Britney was fragile following her divorce from Kevin Federline, and Alli was there to assist with almost everything, even the children. Alli loved to say we were all relatives, but it wasn't the case. Sam exploited Alli, or perhaps she was complicit with him. To this day, I'm not sure. Britney became Sam's target, and he meticulously destroyed her life. Britney's prior team members gradually faded away, and Sam assumed control of everything in my sister's life. He appeared psychotic and manipulative to me. Before Britney went out, he'd phone the photographers. When I questioned him why he did it, he denied it, even though I saw him make the call. Later, he said he did it to relieve Britney's fear of the press. He'd set up meetings with producers and then lie about it. He kept Britney apart from Daddy and Momma. He'd shut them out and deny them access to their grandchildren. He seemed to be constantly looking at properties and attempting to convince Britney to rent various residences in the region. I didn't grasp his significance in her life. When I asked Britney why he was there, she responded she didn't know. Finally, I decided to try to persuade him to go. "What brings you here, Sam?" You should go. Nobody needs your presence here!" "Come on, Jamie Lynn," he said. You seem to enjoy me." I was perplexed. "I do not like you!" I shouted. Even as a sixteen-year-old, I recognized him as a very bad presence in our lives.

Things worsened. I was the only family member who was permitted to enter the house. On my next visit, when I tried once again to get rid of him, he attempted to influence me too. "Good day, Jamie Lynn. I know your parents don't want your boyfriend to visit you in Los Angeles. I've set up a place for you both to stay in. I can find Casper a job where he can earn a lot of money." I looked at him, stunned. "I'm not doing that!" What type of grown-up man gives that to a teen?

Sam's manipulations persisted, and he told her a variety of lies in order to legitimise his exclusive role in her life. I was sceptical of the circumstances. I had the impression that narcotics were easily accessible at the house. Although I never witnessed anything, my sister's strange conduct made me wary. When I visited, I never ate or drank anything for fear that anything had dissolved in her Gatorades and juices.

If you didn't answer a question or ignored him, Sam became infuriated. He was gaining power over Britney, controlling how she spent her time and money. With each visit, I became increasingly concerned. I was young, but not inexperienced. Suspicion grew when I realised that her typical assistants, who arranged appointments and were part of her entourage, had been fired and replaced with some pretty dubious characters. I became really uneasy in the house.

It was clear that she had little influence over many parts of her life. Sam was frightening and clearly had an influence on some of her actions. Britney was nervous, but she sought his praise. He was making appointments with producers he had no right to, and I was obliged to intervene on Britney's behalf at one point. She was uneasy and refused to meet with a producer who had unexpectedly arrived at her home. She dashed upstairs and shut herself in her bedroom. She urged me to get rid of the person through a speakeasy door, which was a little sliding panel in her bedroom door. I reluctantly did as I was instructed, but I noted that her conduct got increasingly irregular over the course of a few weeks. My feeble attempts to remove him from her life left me feeling helpless to assist her.

I knew she'd been through a lot in a short period of time, and I wondered if the mix of stardom, motherhood, and a public divorce had been too much for her, leaving her exposed to negative influences. Her existence was blurry, like if she were seeing through unfocused binoculars. I was sixteen years old and didn't grasp the devils that surrounded my sister; all I knew was that something seemed odd. In actuality, she was having to deal with the impact from Sam's deception. This left her an emotional disaster with no one she could rely on.

After he was removed from Britney's life, he continued to phone me and my family. That just felt like a terrible attempt to stay in our lives. He tried to contact me after I became pregnant with Maddie, but I quickly blocked him. Sam Lutfi, in my opinion, epitomises an insidious society of people who leverage others. They prey on the weak and disabled for personal benefit, taking advantage of anyone who is vulnerable to their attention. And Britney was at her lowest point when he appeared. Unfortunately, Sam Lutfi continues to make ridiculous claims about his time with my sister. He just attempted to enlist Momma in another of his scams. She now has a permanent restraining order against him.

Britney's behaviour became increasingly erratic until it all came to a head. Britney received the assistance she required thanks to my parents' backing. The conservatorship was established at the time, and a restraining order was imposed to protect Britney from Sam. I have little doubt that Sam was the primary cause of my sister's pre-existing emotional anguish. I knew Britney had gone through a lot in the last few years and hoped her downward spiral was only temporary. Britney continued to back me up and be the greatest sister she could be at the time. My sister was blinded by the spotlights, which impaired her capacity to notice the hazards all around her-dangers that still exist. Britney's light was sometimes too strong for me, and I should have done more to protect her.

5.

Pregnancy and Perception

When the credits rolled on the final episode of Zoey 101, I was overcome with emotion. This was the end of an era and a show that altered not only my life, but the lives of all of my castmates and crew members. Everyone was heading in opposite directions, and my compass was spinning. I had several options for continuing to work and expanding my following. What do I do now? What, more television? Movies? Complete high school and then college? Or should I strike while the iron was still hot and I was still relevant? It was a scary and uncertain period, but I relished the opportunity to return home and unwind.

I felt unmoored, with nothing to anchor me professionally or personally. I didn't have a job, and Casper and I had just broken up again. Being a young television celebrity while keeping a good relationship with a distant adolescent guy was challenging to say the least. We were together for a long time, and I was lost in the intense sentiments of first love, or what I thought was love. The barrage of emotions and fear that washed over me made me second-guess my decision to cease seeing him.

Season after season, our relationship grew more serious. I became acquainted with his family, and he became acquainted with mine. He travelled to Los Angeles to be with us, and he even appeared as an extra on the show. But the months apart had an effect. I really liked him, but I wasn't sure how to make a relationship work when I was gone so much. We were battling to stay together by the end of Zoey. There were reports about him spending time with other women, yet when I hung out with male friends, he became furious. I began to doubt whether we were worth fighting for. I knew we had to get back together, or I'd have to figure out how to let him go. We were going in opposite ways, and one of us or both of us needed to change course. After nearly two years together, it became brutally clear that the passion of first love was fading, and I severed it.

I took advantage of a free period in my schedule to get away. Nickelodeon generously provided me with a trip to the Bahamas once we finished the episode. I invited my friend Kasey to join me on the celebratory trip, and I left the world behind to avoid making future decisions. The Bahamians were friendly, and the environment urged us to relax. We had a lovely day relaxing in the sun and taking in the tropical atmosphere. Kasey and I were both conservative, but we both tried the local beer, which neither of us could handle. When we returned to Los Angeles, we spent our time doing everything I'd never had time for while working. We went to the Getty Museum, to the beach, and to a couple famous parties. I'd never been into LA's nightlife, but I figured I'd give it a shot. People were pleasant enough, but I preferred to stay at home.

Breaking up with Casper proved more difficult than I anticipated. We didn't take long to resume texting and talking. I quickly returned to Louisiana and rejoined him. We spent the majority of the week together. Casper persuaded me that we could make it work. We tried to have fun by attending an LSU game. But as soon as I sat in my seat on the plane back to LA, I began to have reservations. The whispers of his cheating on me resumed, becoming increasingly difficult to ignore, and I knew it was all over. It took some time to muster the confidence to break it off, but I eventually did.

My colleagues pushed me to begin the audition process right away. Nickelodeon was encouraging me to pursue new projects, and I was bracing myself for the obstacles that come with change. With my past achievements, I was optimistic about a long-term career in the entertainment world. After another split, I needed some time to recuperate and wasn't quite ready to go into my next endeavour. I spent the majority of my time in the Los Angeles apartment where I lived with my mother, but when I needed space and quality time with my sister, I went to Britney's place. I'd go there all the time just to enjoy the vastness and beauty of the surroundings. The time I spent with her in Malibu allowed us to be sisters in an isolated setting. We were just two regular ladies hanging around and enjoying our sisterly closeness when we were just the two of us. Outside of that, it was difficult to make sense of Britney's universe, and I began to have second thoughts about remaining at her place. There, I grew really uneasy. Britney assured me that everything was fine, and as the younger sister, I trusted her. She convinced me to return to work after a few days together. The entire scene made me uneasy, and I just wanted to get out of there.

I awoke every day for the following three weeks feeling out of sorts. I was feeling sick and all I wanted to do was sleep. I was so exhausted. My irritability increased with time. There was a constant sense of nostalgia and homesickness. Team Jamie Lynn assumed I was just being a typical moody teen and pushed me to keep working. But I had a feeling something was awry. I kept working, appearing on Ashton Kutcher's TV show Miss Guided and reading for movie roles. But my chronic lethargy and sickness finally caught up with me. I walked in to audition for a possible blockbuster film about teen vampires. Twilight's premise sounded totally ludicrous. Walking in, I turned to Momma and said, "This concept doesn't seem like something that people are going to buy into." But I ignored my discomfort, nibbling on crackers to soothe my roiling stomach, and waited my turn. I had a whole chat that I can't remember because I was so dizzy, but I waved to Lily Collins from across the room. Sitting in the waiting room with so many other performers, the sickness and anxiety finally reached a breaking point. I was so unwell that when I was called in, I couldn't give my reading the attention it deserved. My lack of effort was concerning because I was always one for professionalism. I had to leave. It isn't simply the studio. I needed to gather my belongings and return to Louisiana.

My decision to return home relieved my strain, and I believed that my continual concern and fatigue would be lifted. Returning to a comfortable and familiar setting was just what I needed. My life had changed dramatically in a short period of time. Casper and I were officially over, and I felt the strain of being unemployed. Big decisions about my future could be postponed. My aim was to spend some time in my shorts and sweaters, hanging out with pals.

I returned to Kentwood and resumed my life in Momma's house, sleeping in late, catching up with friends, and attending high school instead of the tutoring I had received on set. I got up and arrived at school on time, but my friend Jessica noticed I was dragging. Emotions were getting the best of me, and the nausea wasn't going away. I was still trying to tell myself that it was just the release of tension from working for so long, the end of the play, and the breakup. But when the sickness didn't go away and I discovered I'd missed my period, I began to reflect about the last time Casper and I had been intimate. We hadn't been together in a long time, so I spent days convincing myself that I couldn't be pregnant. Then I remembered the September weekend when I flew in for an LSU game. I could feel the beginnings of panic. This was the first time I actually pondered the prospect of being pregnant.

At first, I was terrified. I panicked and felt a sense of fear that I had never felt before. The fear continued, but as time passed, acceptance began to take root. Jessica and I talked every day, but it took me a while to tell her that something wasn't quite right. We were hanging out at my house when I brought it up, and she asked if I thought I was pregnant. I couldn't say no to the prospect. She went on to say, "Jamie Lynn—I think you really need to take a test."

I was sick with nervousness by the time I put on my shorts and T-shirt. I took the keys to my mother's two-seater Lexus, not realising I was leaving my house for the last time as a child. I couldn't tell you what routes I took or what was on the radio till today. Jessica and I drove around for a long time, unsure what to do. We couldn't possibly stroll into a store to get a pregnancy test without being recognized. I didn't mean people would recognize me, the teen star; I meant it was a small town and anyone we ran into would recognize local kids Jamie Lynn and Jess. Who could I entrust such a delicate matter to? We devised a strategy. My mother was obviously out of the question. She'd freak out. My family knew everyone, and in a tiny town, news spread like wildfire. Just as I was about to pass out, Jess and I remembered our friend Ms. Heidi, who was a few years older than us and lived a few towns away. She had a youthful spirit and enjoyed hanging around with us. We called her and begged her to go to the store, purchase the test, and place it in her mailbox. Ms. Heidi's assistance was quite helpful. At the very least, I wouldn't have to worry about getting caught in the store.

We drove by a little while later and took the test from her mailbox. I swear I thought I was going to puke the moment I got my hands on that test. My rushing heart and racing thoughts made it difficult to concentrate on my driving. We pulled into the BP gas station off Veterans Boulevard out of desperation, knowing it had a single-stall restroom, no keys, no questions, and no interruptions. Jess shut the door, and I did what most females in my situation do: I sat, stuck, and waited.

A universal truth about time exists. It accelerates during good times and crawls during bad times. Those few minutes in the restroom seemed to go forever. I felt as if I were in some strange vortex. Thoughts were bursting like bubbles from a wand. What if... Oh my God! What will my parents think? My father is going to murder him. What will happen to my career? I've always been known as the "good" girl. A baby? Could I become a mother? Everything I've worked for is about to be taken away from me. But a child! I concentrated on the cracks in the floor, the fluorescent lighting, and the muffled sounds from outside to try to stop the flood of thoughts.

As I sat there, so much of the previous several weeks began to make sense. But how was I meant to know what it was like to be pregnant at my age? Jessica was yelling, "He's a dirty dog, your ex–piece of shit." She'd never liked Casper, and now she was cursing him to high heaven for putting me in this situation. She was enraged on my behalf, but I had no capacity for rage in my thoughts.

I was supposed to receive an answer within minutes. The seconds passed, and the anticipation made me queasy as ever. The plastic stick perched on the sink's edge, mocking me, waiting to decide my fate. We were terrified and peered at it from a distance. Oh my God! My life could be eternally altered. My eyes welled up with tears, and I couldn't look. So Jessica, like a good friend, did it for me. She took it up. I'll never forget the look on her face as she looked from me to the positive test and back again, stunned. My world came to a halt in an instant, and I froze. All except one of my previous ideas had vanished: how was I going to face my mother in the eyes and speak the words "I'm pregnant"?

My synapses were firing and I was woozy when the shock wore off. What should I do first? Who should I tell? I chose the obvious option, which was to call Casper and inform him. He wasn't convinced. He assumed it was a ruse.

I said, "A ploy for what?"

He implied that I slept around and that even if I was pregnant, the baby wasn't his. He was the only person I had ever had sexual relations with. Casper was still sceptical. We hung up, and I was stunned. Confused and still feeling wretched, I asked, "What do I do now?"

My inner voice kept telling me that I was going to have a baby. I contacted my close friend Diane from McComb, Mississippi, whose help and quick thinking gave me the assistance I required.

Fortunately, almost everyone in McComb is linked. Diane called a close family friend who was a doctor at McComb OB-GYN Associates. She conveyed my case to Dr. Dawn, and the next morning we met at the clinic's back entrance. My anxiety was heightened by the snooping about. At times, I thought my heart would leap out of my chest. The scene seemed strange, especially when Dr. Dawn motioned toward the examination room. Diane and Jessica waited in another room as the doctor examined me and did an ultrasound, during which I heard my baby's heartbeat for the first time. My tiny "froggy" had a strong heart and a rhythm that lived within me by the time I was seven weeks pregnant. The strange repeated swooshing sound invaded every particle in the room. I felt such awe and an overwhelming sense of peace hearing her heartbeat—as if she was saying, "Momma, Momma, Momma." Then my stomach flipped like I was in a free fall. I intended to become a mother.

It took a few seconds for me to realise Dr. Dawn was speaking to me. "Jamie Lynn, you need to call your momma ASAP," she advised professionally and compassionately. You are a minor and as such your parents need to be notified immediately." My initial reaction was pure panic, followed by hysteria. I wasn't convinced I could pull it off. I considered several approaches to telling her. "Hello, Momma?" What do you think? You're going to be a grandma again." Or, "You're never going to guess what happened to me!"

I regained control and took up the phone to contact her. I tried twice and, thankfully, she did not respond. The Lord had spared me for a short time. I was so relieved that I burst into tears for the second time in two days. I sat silently on the exam table, caressing my flat tummy, and considered the reality of the baby growing inside of me. Dr. Dawn provided additional prenatal information as well as a prescription for prenatal vitamins and an ultrasound of my baby. I spent a long time staring at the image. For me, that visual vision changed my life. My kid was real, and I became a mother at that instant.

After numerous unsuccessful attempts to contact my ex in order to give the official news, we drove around, went to a McDonald's drive-through, and I purchased my first Happy Meal. The chicken nuggets and french fries were wonderful, and the time to digest everything was priceless. I imagined myself as a mother! Jessica was ranting: "Casper... ugh, he's awful... I hate him and what he's done to you... When I get my hands on him..." Diane, on the other hand, was deep in thought. She put it all out there minutes later.

"You know the press is going to get a hold of this story, Jamie Lynn." It will either be 'Child Star Gets Knocked Up and Has an Abortion,' or 'Jamie Lynn Spears Pregnant at Sixteen, No Longer America's Good Girl.' It's media madness no matter what."

I knew it all had to be true. I was terrified of how the rest of the world would react to everything. I was young, famous, single, and pregnant—talk about a media circus. I was essentially hurling a grenade into my carefully crafted career path. Kapow. I put my palm on my belly to attempt to concentrate on my baby. I knew I should be concerned about the pregnancy's consequences, but none of that mattered at the time. I just knew I was going to have my baby, and nothing or no one could change that.

We got back in the car and proceeded to Liberty, Mississippi, where Casper was living with far too many liberties because his father was away on business. He had no one to answer to and spent his days drinking and partying. It was a waste of time to knock on the door. Nobody responded. I was becoming annoyed and thought that we needed to do something extreme to attract Casper's attention. We bought a cheap frame to keep the ultrasound photo from flying away and hung it on the front door. We got in the car and waited for the phone to ring.

Momma was frantic by this point. She was calling all over the place seeking for me, so I had to go home and calm her down. Acting came naturally to me, and she was persuaded everything was alright, but I was terrified on the inside. Casper finally called many hours later, citing all kinds of nonsense, such as, "How do I know the baby is mine?" This sonogram does not even include your name. It's not your test." I tried to explain everything, but my words were jumbled with emotion that made it difficult to speak. It never occurred to me that he would question my honesty. I had never cheated before. I returned to his residence to speak with him in person. I went over the timeline and the facts. Because I was a minor and hadn't been given authorization to do the test, the doctor couldn't write my name on the ultrasound. It took some convincing, but he was finally convinced that the baby was his.

Soon after, we informed his parents, who were pleased with the news. We then went to my house to inform Momma. It didn't matter that we'd broken up or that I was struggling with my emotions. We were expecting, and I was determined to have this baby from the moment I saw that tiny life on the screen and heard the heartbeat. It would happen if I told myself enough times.

He drove us to my house so that we could inform my mother. We got out of the car and proceeded to the front door without saying anything. We just stood there, unable to communicate due to the gravity of the situation. Casper and I were engrossed in our own thoughts and feelings, but I was pleased he was there with me at the time. My internal freak-out continued as we entered the house. The thought of informing Momma was paralysing. I just couldn't say anything.

Instead, I scribbled the words on a note, dropped it in front of her, and fled the room. I dashed to the couch, where I sat next to Casper, in need of his assistance. Then we had to wait. It didn't take long at all.

"DEAR JAMIE LYNN! You're expecting a child? Is this a joke?"

Momma wasn't angry at first, but rather in disbelief. "But we just had to talk about all of that." Her words were bittersweet. "Jamie Lynn, you're my baby, having a baby." It was obvious that worry suffused her tone. Momma first approached Bryan and informed him that there was a problem. Momma had Bryan call Daddy because she was worried about how he would react.

I went to school the day after I told Momma about the baby to keep up appearances. Reality began to sink in gradually. This baby was going to cause havoc in my life. Was I willing to put my career on hold indefinitely, upsetting the team of professionals who had helped me along the way? Would everyone be laid off? It occurred to me that this decision affected a large number of people. That thought made me wonder what might happen. The pregnancy had far-reaching consequences. As a famous performer, I understood the importance of confidentiality, especially in this situation. I knew in my heart that shit would hit the fan, and I needed to keep in touch with the people I trusted. I drove to Walmart after school to get a couple of burner phones.

When I got home from school, Daddy and Bryan were waiting for me. A single day had passed before Daddy's rage heightened everyone's concern about my situation. Things quickly got out of hand after Momma and Daddy informed my team. When I arrived, Daddy, Bryan, and Momma were already there, and Ms. Lou Taylor of Tri Star, my financial management team, was on the phone. There was a whole lot of fighting going on between everyone involved. The entire Spears team was already caught up in my sister's PR difficulties, and everyone around me just wanted to make this "issue" disappear. My family and management removed me from school until they could decide what to do next. They took my smartphone away, fearing the news would get out, and insisted that no one share any information with anyone, especially the press. My daddy and I stopped speaking and the tension was terrible.

For the first few days, I spent most of the time in my room. Everyone had their own opinion about what was best for me. One person after another-and there were many-came to my room trying to convince me that having a baby at this point in my life was a terrible idea. There was lots of chatter, but none of it felt right to me. It will kill your career. You are just too young. You don't know what you're doing. There are pills you can take. We can help you take care of this problem. Think about what you're doing to your family. Doesn't the family have enough to deal with? I know a doctor. There are procedures that remedy mistakes like this. You don't have to do this. He's a louse. He'll never be able to care for the baby or you. Jamie Lynn, don't make a mistake you'll regret for the rest of your life. I'll never forget that last plea-of making a mistake I would regret-because it reinforced my decision to have my baby.

Discussions continued, and everyone was certain that termination would be the best course of action. I will never forget when Ms. Lou stood up for me and said, "Y'all can't force her to abort the baby." She was the first and only person on my team to show any support for my desire to keep my baby. The next option was for me to go to Mercy Ministries, a home for unwed mothers in Tennessee, where I could eventually give up my baby for adoption. Daddy and I fought, slinging words and tossing insults. He grabbed me by the shoulders and held on tightly in the hopes of bending me to his will. I got in his face and yelled, "NO! I won't go." I couldn't deal with any of them. I ran away from them, painting with rage.

Despite my decision to have my baby, I struggled with self-loathing, guilt, and panic. I was smart enough to know that I was essentially a child, having a baby. But childhood would fade quickly as Froggy grew in my belly. I knew this situation was going to derail my career, and I knew that my parents were ashamed of me. I'd spent my entire life trying to be the perfect daughter, performer, and professional. I was always under so much pressure to make everyone's life easier, including my own. I was all things to all people. Now, the pressure to maintain that image and manage the disappointment was suffocating. With all the chaos surrounding my sister, I never wanted to be a burden to my family. My family had their own version of what was right. With the pregnancy, my sense of right became the opposite of theirs. I needed help figuring out what to do. Those burner phones came in handy. I periodically changed the SIM cards for security and spoke with the few friends who supported me.

I remained sequestered, while preventing a press leak became my team's priority. Contracts were drafted and nondisclosures signed by Casper and anyone who might try to benefit from releasing the story. My team, who I realised had a difficult time supporting my decision, still managed to help me move through the myriad of business concerns. Daddy took off to California to be with my sister and Momma-well, she was there. I agreed to cut an exclusive deal with OK! magazine to release the pregnancy story and the first pictures of me and my baby to the world. It was the only way I felt I could have some control over the situation. Social media wasn't the platform it is today, and everyone felt that an exclusive deal would be the best way to tell my story. If this had happened to me once social media became the all-consuming medium it is today, my experience would have been different. Some of my trauma may have been avoided, but the onslaught of the world weighing in with their thoughts and opinions would have been even more damaging. Social media will always be a double-edged sword; it can defend and inform, just like it can damage and destroy.

The transaction had very little to do with money at the time, and everything to do with controlling the possible media storm. My team planned for someone to guide me through the process, but the pregnant article ended up being a mix of coached responses and my own honest sentiments.

Without a smartphone or internet access, home seemed like a prison. My squad believed that everyone outside of the inner circle posed a threat. They even went so far as to keep my pregnancy a secret from my sister, arguing that "it's too risky to tell Britney about the baby." I needed her more than ever, and she was unable to assist me during my most vulnerable period. Britney's health was becoming increasingly serious. They were afraid that her insecurity at the moment rendered her untrustworthy. I did what my team ordered me to do because I was a youngster and didn't want to cause any more problems. Britney found out about the pregnancy after the article was published. The pain of not being able to tell my sister myself persists to this day.

I was still suffering from morning sickness, which drained me of any energy I had at the moment. I was exiled and essentially hidden away. Loneliness and misery remained. Those feelings were heightened when the team determined that Momma and I should be relocated from our home to a secure location far away until OK! published the story. This irritated me, but I couldn't muster the courage to disagree. My mother and I were escorted by our security team to an undisclosed location in Connecticut. We flew into New York and then travelled for what seemed like an eternity. I'm still not sure where we hid in the Northeast.

Thanksgiving 2007 was spent in a modest cabin, far away from the traditions that the holiday had inspired. There was no home-cooked lunch with family and friends. Morning nausea turned into an all-day problem. The cold was severe, preventing us from even sitting outside. It was unbearable to stay in that cabin. Momma wore her displeasure like a beloved garment, and only Sugar, my bearlike and adoring security guard, offered me genuine care. I'll never forget the several movies he made sure I had to keep me entertained, or the gold-encrusted "Mom" necklace he gave me at that terrible time. I locked myself in the cabin's bathroom and called Diane, who was away on holiday, on one of my burner phones. Despite not knowing the number, she answered. "Diane. Hello, my name is Jamie Lynn. I'm terrified. They relocated me somewhere freezing. And all I can tell you is that it's snowing. There isn't anything for miles!" We talked for a few minutes longer, and just hearing her voice helped.

We were informed that the OK! issue was complete. The piece, which was published in December 2007, received massive media attention. The pregnancy announcement was covered by every newspaper. Even by today's standards, the headlines were harsh: "Pregnant Jamie Lynn Spears Not Much of a Role Model." The television coverage was also excruciating. "Jamie Lynn-no future!" , "Her life is over!" , and even "She has no idea what she's gotten herself into." Again, I consider myself fortunate that Instagram, Facebook, and Twitter were still in their early stages at the time. My pregnancy and the period of the filming of Zoey 101 sparked speculation. The media constantly vilified my character and speculated on whether Nickelodeon would telecast the show's final season. To this day, many people believe Zoey 101 ended because of me or that my pregnancy had an impact on the show. That could not be further from the truth. The final episode of Zoey was shot months before I found out I was pregnant. When the news of my pregnancy became public, Nickelodeon backed me up in my decision. The execs were just concerned about my safety. We maintain a professional and respectful connection, and I will be eternally grateful for their trust in me and my family's support.

My baby and I made headlines. Travelling through airports was not an option. We hid for a few more days before driving the twenty-two hours back to Kentwood to evade the paparazzi. The cabin was unpleasant enough, but the hours spent caged up in that car were unbearable. I was tired and tried to sleep most of the way home. And the solitude persisted. This was a difficult period for me. I tried not to worry what Hollywood thought of me. I still felt obligated to be a positive role model for girls. I wasn't "America's sweetheart" or "a young person with the potential to change the world" any longer; instead, adjectives like "slut," "disgrace," and "disappointment" were used to describe me. Every headline embarrassed and humiliated my family and me. There was no press support, and my tale became an invitation for any media outlet and random individual to believe they knew who I was, what my intentions were, or had any notion of what was going on in my life. At sixteen, it was difficult for me to make sense of anything, let alone the changes in my body and circumstances. No one on the team listened to me, and every time I tried to speak up, I was stymied. This situation felt oppressive, and I began to consider dramatic measures.

I studied for my GED and thought about my possibilities. Everything has to be changed. I was frantic to figure out how to support myself and the baby in this new existence. I finally felt better during my second trimester of pregnancy, and my brain was able to handle things more effectively. Nobody ever tells you that the agony of chronic morning sickness makes normal functioning impossible. The respite enabled me to take better care of myself and enjoy my pregnancy more. I deliberated and devised a strategy. My friends stood by me and helped me stay sane. The paparazzi didn't make it easy for me and followed me around constantly.

It was creepy to have dozens of middle-aged males following me around all the time. They followed us several times as we went shopping at a neighbourhood store. Some of the most heinous photojournalists would yell at me, "Aren't you ashamed of yourself, Jamie Lynn?" "How does it feel to be a letdown?" As many as ten people followed me around as I ran errands and went to doctor's appointments. They uploaded images of the clinic where I had my prenatal exams. The fact was that going anywhere was exhausting, and sitting at home was claustrophobic.

While I was deciding what to do next, my parents tried to persuade me that Casper should remain my ex-boyfriend. They said I was living in a fantasy world if I expected him to be a caring and supporting partner. That I needed to get a handle on reality or he'd wreck everything I'd fought so hard for. They might have been correct, but I wasn't ready to concede that Casper was a bad guy-not even to myself. I wasn't having it at the time. I was so preoccupied with creating the ideal life for Casper and our child. They had little faith in my abilities to create a happy and healthy environment for myself. Their cause shifted from the baby to the financial security of my future.

Ms. Lou Taylor had stood firm in my defence during the upheaval. She had joined my staff two years before, and I had grown to trust her to look after my best interests. Ms. Lou, on the other hand, had a vested interest in keeping me lucrative. Ms. Lou became a mentor to me as my pregnancy proceeded, teaching me financial planning and budgeting to keep me sustainable. Previously, I had no say over how much money I made or how it was invested. But now everything has changed, and as much as I would have appreciated a supporting partner during this difficult time, Casper was unconcerned about the future. Don't get me wrong: he enjoyed the perks of being in my life; he just didn't want the responsibility.

I went to my friends once more, notably Diane, who assisted me in sorting through the difficulties I needed to overcome and establishing myself as a strong independent young lady. She and I had multiple discussions on the burner phones, building a long-term plan. She assisted in arranging a meeting with a Hammond lawyer who was not part of the team to identify steps to emancipate myself and take control of my life and finances. Too many people were telling me what was best for me, and I wanted to make my own choices. My impressionable heart had already weaved thoughts of a home where Casper and I could raise our baby and prove we could be happy when I was sixteen. The only way that could happen quickly was for me to leave under my parents' roof and be on my own. This idea was met with immediate opposition from all sides. My parents believed I was being dumb, and my brother, Bryan, was saddened that I was making such important decisions at such a young age. Britney was dealing with her own issue, and because we were separated, contact was nonexistent. My family rejected my attempts at independence, leaving me with no choice except to threaten the courts with emancipation. I agonized for days over my impending decision. But I went with my instincts and told my new lawyer to draft the petition. My lawyer and I came up the next Saturday morning and served papers on my mother. Daddy had already left, so Momma contacted the team to discuss the problems. They were really concerned about me marrying my partner and giving him full access to my earnings. At the same time, my sister was having her own breakdown, and media conjecture about her health and our family had the photographers crawling. Everyone engaged in my saga grudgingly agreed that we needed to do anything we could to avoid further unwanted media attention.

6.

Breaking Up and Letting Go

It was strange to me to try to acquire freedom by threatening Momma with emancipation papers. However, I needed everyone to take my concerns seriously, and this appeared to be, my only option. Momma stood there in surprise when my lawyer and I arrived to serve her. We were probably both thinking the same thing: How did this happen? We waited for Momma to call the lawyers and consult with my team. Finally, they determined to go to whatever length to defend me. Emancipation would put my personal and financial well-being at danger, something no one wanted. We threw away the emancipation papers, and I was granted my freedom. Our agreement gave me the authority to handle my own affairs and make decisions for myself and my child. My parents would still be my legal guardians, with the right to intervene if I made bad judgments. I had no intention of complicating an already precarious situation. I felt in my heart that I was making the right decision, but independence came at a cost.

The day's events were emotionally draining, and our mutual discomfort made it hard for me to stay in the house any longer. Momma wanted me to stay with her and assist me in navigating the next year of my life. But I just knew that if Casper and I were to stay together and raise our child, I needed to get out from under her roof. Even if Momma's intentions were genuine, I would never be able to assert myself and grow into the mother I desired to become while living there. I marched to my room, holding my head high, and stuffed everything I could into large rubbish bags. The soiled plastic bags piled into my Range Rover were a sight to behold. I drove out to Liberty to stay with Casper's family.

He made genuine attempts to be helpful at first. But we were young, and Casper was more concerned with his pals and having a good time. Sometimes he'd say exactly what I wanted to hear, but I'm not sure he was interested in taking on the burden of creating a life with me. Casper's prior misdeeds had weakened my faith in him, regardless of how much I loved him. I had a sneaking suspicion he wasn't good for me or the baby, but Momma wouldn't have agreed to let me move out if she believed I'd be on my own. In my young heart, I honestly hoped it would be the start of a new chapter in our relationship. Now that the most difficult decisions had been made, I felt obligated to prove to the public that I could do it-to be the "perfect" adolescent mom who made it work while maintaining a stable relationship with her boyfriend. We weren't about to become a statistic. We intended to start a family for our daughter.

I went to great lengths to demonstrate my loyalty to him. We "played house" at his parents' house, pretending to be a family. I knew I wanted my own place from the start, but we agreed that a few weeks at his would give us time to plan. He used to work as a welder, but he stopped shortly after I moved in. I discovered a small bag of pills while cleaning a few weeks later. I didn't identify them and flushed them down the toilet without thinking. He freaked out when I contacted him and casually indicated that I'd gotten rid of some drugs I found in a baggie. He was furious, claiming they belonged to a friend of his. Concerned, I approached his mother, inquiring about his habits, and she basically replied, "Boys will be boys." Ribbons of suspicion began to unfold. One strike.

Life in that house was not good for me, but my pride dictated that I smile for the sake of the world. I created a role that I played for everyone out of need. "Happy Jamie Lynn" wore a mantle of contentment that obscured the tension and unease I felt on a regular basis. Casper's parents were friendly, but their permissive nature made me uneasy, and we never became close. Casper couldn't possibly join me in cultivating a healthy family life for us if he never had to take responsibility for himself. I didn't like the paparazzi spreading rumours about my relationship, and I didn't want to hear "I told you so" from my parents. It was simply easier to act as if everything was fine. I became increasingly self-conscious in his home and realized that I desperately needed my own space. It was time to leave. After a difficult talk with my management in which I justified the cost of a new home, I contacted a Realtor and began looking at houses.

The Liberty property I chose was in the middle of nowhere. In retrospect, that was probably not my greatest decision. It was a swift cash transaction, and I promptly erected a high fence to ensure my privacy and the safety of my growing baby. The press continued to torment me, but at least I was safe in my own home. I was nesting because of the pregnancy. I was building our house together from the ground up, from the paint and appliances to the curtains and amenities. This was challenging for a variety of reasons. Primarily because I was a child with nothing to call my own.

Casper spent most of his days doing who knows what, except when it came to furnishing our home with the latest computer toys and televisions money could buy. He insisted on a camouflage-themed room, complete with camo bedding, to show his hunting photographs. In an effort to make him happy, I agreed to most of his suggestions. We were looking around our house one morning when he observed, "You know, Jamie Lynn, these floors aren't going to sweep themselves." That is something you must do." I couldn't believe he said that and thought to myself, "I'm paying for all of this!" You're the one who sweeps the floors. What did I really know about sweeping? I had no prior experience with housekeeping. Previously, if I wasn't working, I was either at school, church, or participating in sports. He never used a broom or vacuum, but he took advantage of any opportunity to spend money. I did my best to provide us with all we required while dealing with my morning sickness and running my business. I had work opportunities that needed to be postponed, and I needed to rethink my financial strategy to keep us afloat. When I was fatigued from the day, he went out late into the evening to party with friends, and he didn't come home many evenings.

Ms. Lou and I continued to strengthen our friendship, and she was a huge assistance to me in these early months. I knew she was someone on whom I could rely. Her assistance was crucial, especially at a time when my relationship with my parents was just beginning to improve. Ms. Lou's assertiveness appealed to me and, to be honest, was refreshing. Her forceful and dynamic nature came in handy when I realized that most of the ladies in my family struggled to stand their ground and make smart decisions for themselves. She came to see how I was doing and made sure I had all I needed to improve the quality of my everyday life. She went to make a cup of coffee and realized she didn't have a coffee machine. When I told her the nearest coffee shop was eight miles away, she scoffed. I had a French press within hours, and she assisted me in making a house a home. Ms. Lou made decor and style advice and even delivered a picture from my parents' collection for Maddie's nursery. She gasped when she saw Casper's camouflage room. "Come on, Jamie Lynn," she said without hesitation. Let's get some things to polish up the decor here."

Ms. Lou and I built a rapport that went far beyond professional, despite her lack of children and my specific requirements at the time. I knew she wanted to assist me in any way she could to reduce the stress in my life. I appreciated having someone in my corner whose sole responsibility was to prioritise my business concerns and advise me on how to safeguard my future. But, in the process, she put herself in a situation that made Momma uncomfortable. On one level, she helped to heal my family's wounds by soothing them. But I had the impression that Momma was troubled by the intimacy Ms. Lou and I enjoyed.

No one could ever replace Momma in my life, but the previous months, filled with fear, disillusionment, and guilt, had strained our connection. Momma was conflicted; she wanted to do what she thought was best for me while also supporting my decisions. And the truth is that not all of my decisions were sound. Momma was always there for me, even when things were bad. Throughout my upbringing, I was taught that being a Spears meant being strong-willed, vocal, and, most importantly, forgiving whenever possible. Grudges serve no one, and it's a blessing that we may disagree while still caring passionately for each other. I was raised to respect my parents and do what they said at all costs. But, with Froggy on the way, I began to see a significant gap between how I saw my family and the one I envisioned for myself. When I decided to leave my mother's house, I realized that in myself. I didn't resent or blame them for the way I left the house at the time. I realized I had to forge my own path. Momma and Ms. Lou, on the other hand, were guiding figures in my life, including coordinating the deal for Momma's book Through the Storm: A Real Story of Fame and Family in a Tabloid World. Even to this day, I haven't read that book. I saw firsthand the hardships that Momma and Britney faced after my sister read it, and I wanted to avoid any indignation that reading her comments may cause.

The geographical seclusion of the house I lived with Casper strained my relationships with several of my friends. I couldn't hang out with them on a regular basis and provide the continual communication that teenagers require. I was going in a different direction, and we didn't have much in common at the time. My life became a delicate balancing act between sustaining my romantic relationship and my health. I wanted to think that Casper and my love would blossom. We had some pleasant times, but not many, and his adultery grew more difficult to overlook. I somehow convinced myself that if I just tried harder, I could make him happy. I ignored my fears and was genuinely pleased when he proposed to me in March 2008. Okay, now everything will be OK, I reasoned. The ring confirmed my belief that everything would work out. The diamond persuaded everyone else that we were content. The interaction established our credibility in the eyes of the rest of the globe. I was doing the best I could for my child.

This entire setup was designed to shore up my sagging public reputation. I was still striving to be the wonderful person everyone had come to adore, proving that this pregnancy wasn't the disaster it had been reputed to be. In actuality, my fiancé was gone more than he was home, and his whereabouts were mostly unknown to me.

Some days, I wished I could be with him. However, wanting that and feeling safe in our relationship were not the same thing. I just knew something wasn't right at the time. He wasn't behaving normally. When I questioned where he'd been, he ignored me, saying things like, "Your hormones are driving you insane." I had left. We're just hanging out. Despite the ring, trust was slipping through my fingers like sand. Strike number two.

Momma and I's relationship improved as the strain between us dissipated over time. Momma was overjoyed to have a lavish baby shower for me at her home after everything we'd been through. I despised being the focus of attention, but I couldn't turn her down. According to rumors, I had a "redneck, half-assed" baby shower. With all that had happened in the previous seven months, all of the media coverage and negative press, I felt it was critical that people see the lovely celebration commemorating my pregnancy. In another attempt to control the narrative and what the public saw, I hired a family acquaintance to photograph the events of the day. The photographs, which were of poor quality, were sold to OK! magazine to write an article. Reporters continued to swarm that day, even flying helicopters over the yard. Everything they did was intrusive, and I felt violated in such a private setting. I put on that "Happy Jamie Lynn" smile, but I could feel a crack in my veneer. Diane arranged a smaller shower a few weeks later, attended by a few close friends, where I could relax and enjoy the excitement of imminent parenting.

My due date was approaching, and the clock was ticking. My skin had stretched beyond belief, and I felt enormous. I was unaware of the hormonal changes that occur during pregnancy. I stupidly assumed that all of my weariness and emotional troubles would go away after the first trimester. I most likely had prenatal depression but had no idea it existed at the time. I was overwhelmed and did everything I could to handle my anxiousness. I remained busy at home, trying to divert my attention away from what was going to happen. I didn't have the option of waiting for natural labour to begin. In order to govern the events of the day, an action plan for the baby's birth was created. To ensure privacy and security during the delivery, an elaborate pretense was used.

I awoke on June 19, 2008, just like any other day, only this time I was going to meet my kid. I took a shower and washed my hair. My youthful vanity had me straightening my hair and curling my bangs to my liking. Casper and I took the 5:00 a.m. bus to the hospital. The appointment time kept the journalists and bystanders in the dark. After we arrived, I went through the standard admissions processes, which were tough for me to focus on because I was about to become a first-time mother. To begin the induction process, I changed into the provided gown. My entire family was supposed to arrive on private jets, which alerted the photographers. Because this was my first child, physicians advised Momma that it would be hours before I gave birth, allowing the family to take their time arriving at the hospital. Things moved slowly at first, and I tried to be as relaxed as possible. Even nevertheless, the morning was filled with drama, and things proceeded far faster than anyone imagined. I was strolling around to relieve some of the pain. The realization hit me all at once. Oh my goodness! I'm expecting a child. I strolled inside the birthing room, cupping my big belly and taking in my surroundings. I started sweating and then puked in an instant. Fetal monitors were implanted on my tummy, and I was feeling contractions unknowingly. Maddie decided not to keep us waiting for very long. My baby had already entered the world by the time the Pitocin kicked in. Casper stood by my side, but the delivering experience was incredibly personal to me. Maddie Briann was born at 9:33 a.m. after much struggling and pushing. Her presence comforted me, and as I held her, a communication flowed between us. We've got it! The fear vanished at that instant, and everything was well in my world.

While I was interacting with Maddie, I couldn't help but notice the odd components all about us. State troopers were stationed outside my door and near the elevators. The number of reporters outside was incredible. Nurses and doctors tried to enter at different times, and I soon discovered that they were reporters dressed up to obtain access. Maddie was not permitted to leave the room. All of her initial examinations and inspections were performed at her bedside. Throughout it all, I felt like Maddie and I were facing our new world. Every time I held her, I felt whole, as if all my pieces had clicked into place. Maddie was an expert at latching on for feedings and made breastfeeding a breeze. Casper was pleased, but took advantage of my post-delivery joy to request a new truck. "You know, Jamie Lynn, so I can drive the baby in a safer vehicle." I had already purchased him a truck, and his request hit me like a punch in the gut. He'd lost any sense of decency. What a shit! I thought. But I did purchase him another vehicle, and after he put on big rims and lifted the cab twenty inches, I couldn't even get Maddie in her car seat. This was yet another Casper deception that contributed to our downward spiral. Fortunately, Maddie's entrance provided solace to my own family, and everyone, including Momma, Daddy, Bryan, and Britney, were overjoyed. All of us in that room, swooning over the newest arrival, provided me peace-at least for a brief while. I was overjoyed that my sister had recovered from her previous breakdown and could join in on the fun.

The parking lot was packed with reporters, and we knew bringing Maddie home would be a logistical headache. The second element of Mission Maddie was a decoy strategy to divert the journalists one way and Maddie the other. The difficulty was that in order for the plan to work, I would have to let her out of my sight. The very concept of someone holding her, let alone giving her to someone else, was scary. But I'd go to any length to keep her safe. I agreed to the ruse against my better judgement. It was getting late in the evening. I sat in a wheelchair after being clothed and ready, and baby Maddie was placed in my hands. We started the long walk downstairs to the car. I was accompanied by a four-person trooper team, and before we got to the lobby, I handed Maddie to one of the troopers, and an identical newborn bundle was placed on my lap. I was rolled out, and a makeshift tunnel was built to protect us and keep the cameras away. I kept my head down and walked slowly into the car. I shut the door and slid the pretend baby bundle into the car seat. I took a big breath and hoped Maddie and the troops were on their way home safely. Words cannot express how relieved I was to have Maddie back in my arms.

My family resumed their own lives a few days after Maddie and I arrived home, and my fiancé was back partying and vanishing for hours. Although his actions irritated me, the precious time I spent with my kid made everything better. His absence allowed Maddie and I to strengthen our bond, and I developed a fondness for breastfeeding. I'd heard about the benefits of breastfeeding before she arrived, but I never realized how reciprocal it would be. Nothing compares to the physical bond between mother and child. It is much more than just nutrition. I like the dynamic of her just needing me; of being the only one who could care for her in this way. Knowing Maddie would return to the safety of my arms every few hours gave me an extra piece of mind. We comforted each other and enjoyed a sense of calm. I spent months breastfeeding my daughter and cherishing that once-in-a-lifetime bliss.

But being a new mother was also a huge challenge. The exhaustion and mood swings subsided soon, but it took some time for me to mentally arrange all of the changes that occurred immediately after Maddie arrived. Lack of sleep, bouts of screaming, sometimes by both of us, and the first few nights on my own, as with so many new parents, made my early days of mothering difficult. I cleared my head and concentrated on our requirements. In Maddie's care, I became hypervigilant and devised a schedule. I ate, slept, and washed at the same times that she did. We were like one entity. It was one of the ways I kept things under control.

The disappearances of Casper raised new questions about our future. The paparazzi pursued my tale relentlessly, and state troopers remained on our property at all hours. Mr. Scott, a state trooper whose children were classmates of mine, was so worried that his wife prepared food for me. I am grateful to him for his fatherly care throughout that period.

I completed my second OK! requirement about nine days after Maddie was born. I was featured in a magazine and sat for a photo session with Maddie. The deal, negotiated months previously, ensured that I retained some control over what was made public. With this exclusive arrangement, my motivation was to keep Maddie as safe as possible. For the most part, the strategy succeeded in reducing the hysteria of the "first photos," and I couldn't wait to get it over with and get on with my life. The shoot was as enjoyable as a new mother could hope for. Maddie was an angel, and we captured some lovely photos that were published in the magazine. I was grateful for the money the images brought in once the project was finished. I'd worked for years to maintain a consistent paycheck. I had no notion what lay ahead for me professionally. The funds would be used to support us in the future and would be held in trust.

Although photographers and media persons continued to attempt to capture photographs from a distance for a few months, the frenzy gradually subsided.

Casper's behaviour deteriorated during the summer. When we initially brought Maddie home, he complained about the curfew recommended by the troopers to keep us safe. When I asked him where he was going or where he'd been, he'd simply say, "Out." Our relationship had been falling apart for months, and I believed he was doing things he shouldn't. He was moody, and his entire personality appeared to shift. He'd been gaslighting me, being evasive and acting as if I was the insane one before Maddie was born. At times, I questioned my own sanity. "Jamie Lynn, I think the pregnancy is making you a little crazy." Granted, I know a lot more about how my body changes during pregnancy now than I did then. Even if I was grumpy, I wasn't a moron. Casper made fun of me and challenged me not to believe him. He was rebellious and became enraged when I called him out on his "overindulging," but now he was just obvious in his behaviour, without even attempting to deceive me or conceal his activities.

I realized I was a new mom, and I had changed as well. However, most of his decisions reflected his disinterest, lack of fatherly concern, and disrespect for our needs. The small amount of faith I had in him, the expectation that he would prioritize me and Maddie in his life, had evaporated by the time fall turned into winter. Rumors about him and other women began to circulate. I was so preoccupied with becoming a mother that I didn't notice the whispers half the time. But I knew Casper was disrespecting me and ignoring Maddie with his actions. Even yet, he would continue to feed me lies about loving me. He would occasionally threaten to leave us if I didn't give in to his petty requests for one item or another. He was skilled at manipulating me, and I was frantic to keep up appearances.

He begged me to invest in his future by funding his schooling. My adviser objected, but I insisted on doing it. Two large sums were deposited into an account for him to use, but the funds vanished within weeks. He dropped out of college. Despite this, he insisted on his love for me. The simple reality is that Casper was only interested in being with me for the money and everything that came with it. At the time, I couldn't see it, and we continued to live in a toxic relationship. I was oblivious and didn't know any better. It was impossible to see the reality of the situation since there was so much upheaval.

Ms. Lou came to see me particularly to sit me down and tell me some hard truths. She wasn't happy with how things were going with Casper and felt she wanted to get me thinking about my future. "All right, Jamie Lynn. What are you going to do to make ends meet, and what kind of legacy do you want to leave Maddie?"I felt like I'd been punched in the stomach." Ms. Lou didn't play games. She was direct and aggressive in her delivery. And the reality was, she had a stake in the game. She was paid if I worked. But she wasn't entirely wrong. When she went, I sat in my living room, staring into space, trying to calm down. I'd never had to think about this before. Money was easy to come by before Maddie. I had planned to continue performing on television before venturing into film. But now I'd essentially wrecked my career and the consistent money that went with it. She offered me a lot to ponder. I had sown the seeds, but they needed time to germinate.

I wrapped my figurative protective cloak over Maddie. Being her mother and witnessing her development brought me such joy that it was sometimes difficult to ignore Casper's actions. Unfortunately, as the months passed, it became clear that the majority of the allegations about girls and substance misuse were most likely genuine. Aside from caring for Maddie, my life became a frantic game of whack a mole, with one media fire after another. There were days when acute anxiety crippled me and the dread of what was to come brought me to tears. To protect myself, I started using birth control, and the transition was difficult. Casper accused me of being hormonally insane and unstable once more. In retrospect, I wonder whether he said that to blame me for his supposed infidelities.

When my team discovered that Casper's paramour was selling her story to the press, the speculation about his transgressions became fact. Within days, a front-page item would surface, increasing my mortification and repugnance. I felt disgusted not only with him, but also with myself. My team, the same people who tried to shield me from him, were forced to reveal the article's precise contents to me. Hearing the truth about Casper's infidelity in that manner remains one of the most embarrassing events of my life to this day. I let him take my hard-earned money, manipulate my emotions, and undermine my self-esteem. I was left feeling deeply ashamed. And I still couldn't admit to anyone how horrible things were at the time. I communicated frequently with my sister and fraudulently persuaded my family that everything was fine. I was doing what I always did: convincing everyone that life was good. My inner thoughts weren't strong enough to overcome my dread of public perception. I craved acceptance, and leaving would mark me as a failure. But, for the first time, I felt as if I were outside of myself, peering down at the life I was leading. I wondered if there was anything else Maddie and I could do.

Maddie's lovely presence and gentle nature inspired her to continue the farce. However, Maddie and I began spending the most of our time with my entire family. We came to Los Angeles together to have a joint birthday party for my nephews and had a fantastic time. We went on tour with Britney, and the time away provided me with a long perspective. I realized I was more than just dissatisfied; I was living in an emotionally abusive home, and my vivacity was slowly dwindling.

When we got home from our trip, I started making modifications. I fired my entire crew, including my manager, who was also my brother's fiancée. Despite the fact that my future business goals were on hold, I continued to devote myself to Maddie's care. My friends, whom I had previously neglected, returned to my life, and spending time with them was rejuvenating. Having wonderful people in my life had a significant impact on me, and my insecurity quickly faded.

I made one more attempt to aid Casper by contacting his family. They proceeded to dismiss my claims and dismissed me. I wasn't going to contribute to his bad behavior any longer. New reports of infidelity and alleged drug usage have surfaced. His interest in Maddie waned with time, and my concern for her safety grew crippling. I couldn't tell what he was thinking, and the thought that his actions might hurt her became a continuous worry. I would never put my daughter in danger. Three strikes.

I went with family and religion. I reached deep into my reservoir of fortitude. I finally admitted that I needed to do better, to make better decisions for myself and Maddie. I made preparations to return to my mother's place while I sorted myself out. I thought we were starting a new life.

The call came late one April night. After years of fretting that the cops might show up at my house, his sister called to tell me that Casper had been in a vehicle accident while attending his cousin's bachelor party. My fiancé had flipped his truck and sustained serious injuries in the short time between my heroic decision and the moment I planned to notify him. I followed my instincts in that moment, unsure how to manage my mixed emotions of fear, irritation, and incredulity. And I was obligated to stay near him for a variety of reasons. He was Maddie's father, and even though I didn't envision a future for our family, I had faith in basic human goodness. I'd put my rage aside and find the strength to be there for him during his recuperation. To be completely honest, I was worried about how the media would portray this new development if I left: "Jamie Lynn,

Heartless Teen Star, Abandons Fiancé After Car Crash" or "Insensitive Spears Leaves Her Baby's Daddy in Crisis." I hadn't gone through years of anguish and sacrificed my self-respect to protect my public image only to have it destroyed now. I would wait until Casper was back on his feet, no matter how terrible it was.

That decision, while taken quickly, was troublesome. I had already checked out of the relationship and was on my way. I found it difficult to care for him because I was filled with fury and frustration. His betrayal and neglect had made me resentful of the care I had to provide. He knew I wouldn't abandon him in such a tough situation, and as his condition improved, he took advantage of my generosity. My displeasure and bitterness got more as he grew stronger.

Casper used pain medicine significantly more than was necessary as a result of the accident. As far as I could tell, he was a very fortunate man to be alive, and he might use this opportunity to get back on track. He, however, did not. Maddie and I stayed for months while dad regained his strength, but the old patterns of duplicity and daylong disappearances quickly reappeared. Maddie and I spent time with my friends when the situation grew unbearable. My sister's tour provided us with an excuse to leave town when we wanted to get away. Our lives improved as we spent more time apart from Casper. My inner strength grew alongside Maddie's. We were entitled to more than an absentee father.

When life in Liberty became too much for Maddie and me, we would spend a few days at Mama's place. She was always welcoming, and the respite from the insanity allowed me to gain more perspective. I enjoyed spending time with my good friends Brandi and Diane, as well as my extended family. I was happier, and Maddie relished the fact that she was surrounded by people who loved her. We were both meeting new people and experiencing new joys.

My cousin Laura Lynn's baby shower was being hosted by the Mitchells. (The Mitchells were the parents of Brandi's boyfriend, Dane.) Dane and Brandi went by at the end of the afternoon to say hello. They arrived in a black Escalade, and I stepped forward to see inside. They were sipping snowballs, a type of shaved ice dessert. I was standing there in my grey turtleneck dress, Maddie on my hip. "Jamie Lynn, this is Jamie Watson," Brandi said. I knew Jamie was Dane's best buddy, but not much else. He said hello. That was my first meeting with him, and I didn't think much of it. I knew who Jamie was because of chats with Brandi. She began to mention him more after that introduction. Jamie had founded his own IT company, which had developed swiftly, and he was well-known in town for being a successful self-starter. His job brought him all across the country, and I could identify with his nomadic, independent lifestyle. I appreciated Jamie being an adult who had his sh*t together at a time when my fiancé was obsessed with finding his next addiction. Brandi kept hinting that he was someone I should get to know, but my mind wasn't in the right place. Jamie would appear more and more frequently whenever I went to see Brandi. But I didn't give it much thought.

Brandi texted me a few weeks later to swing by Dane's on my way home. I pulled up alongside Momma and Maddie. Jamie and Dane were putting up a show while working out. Jamie was clearly attempting to impress me, but he'll deny it! We smiled and said hello to each other. The entire interaction lasted less than five minutes, and I drove away thinking about all the problems I was having with Casper.

I realised I needed a few days away from Casper and the loneliness of Liberty once more. Maddie and I returned to Momma's. I started spending a lot of time with Brandi and her friends. It was pleasant to be around interesting people from many walks of life who had careers and goals. They were older than me, but our age differences didn't matter because of my personal experiences. The more time I spent with Brandi, Dane, and their friends, the more disconnected I felt from my life in Liberty. But I returned within a few days.

After flying in early October, I developed excruciating congestion and injured eardrums. As a result of these difficulties, extensive sinus surgery was required. Momma was in charge of Maddie, and Casper was in charge of bringing me and my meds home after the procedure. He managed to get me into bed, then took some of my pain relievers and left to go party with his pals. I was so out of it that his actions didn't bother me. Momma was enraged.

I was quite sick and in a lot of discomfort after the surgery because of an annoying drip that flowed down my throat. I reflected on how Casper had effectively abandoned me and felt even more animosity after everything I had done for him. I recovered for a few more days and began to feel more like myself. Brandi and I were on our way to a friend's wedding when she asked if I would accompany her to New Orleans for a work function for Dane and Jamie. "I don't want to be the lone girl, Jamie Lynn. And you know Jamie truly likes you." I tried not to think about her last remark too much and concluded that a night out was exactly what I needed. Jamie drove us there in his Porsche, which I believe he did to impress me. Sports cars were not my cup of tea. They are still not. I greatly prefer a large, roomy truck. We spent the entire drive casually talking. Jamie and I had a terrific time at the party, fooling about and daring one other to do ridiculous things. I believe Jamie and I saw each other for the first time. Not the kid actress or the wealthy businessman, but our true selves. It was the first time I'd ever gone out for the sole purpose of having fun, and as platonic as it looked, I kept worrying if I was doing something wrong. Casper and I weren't together, but we weren't divorced either.

Momma, Maddie, Casper, and I flew to New York for Thanksgiving to celebrate with my brother and his family. I was still feeling the effects of the sinus surgery, and Maddie had a cold. Casper was simply unhappy. He was no longer enjoying spending time with us, and it was clear he didn't want to be here. He was moaning and asked if we could shorten the journey. I texted Brandi, "I have to get out of here." It's dreadful. He's depressed, and so am I. I just can't stand it any longer. When I returned to Louisiana, I realised our relationship wasn't working. Despite the fact that we'd split up, I shipped out the family Christmas cards I'd ordered in October, hoping in vain to keep up appearances.

I learned I needed my wisdom teeth pulled just a few weeks into my sinus recuperation. Momma wanted Maddie and I to stay at her place for the entire month of December so she could help me recuperate and we could enjoy the holidays. The treatment went well, and I recovered for a few days. Mother Nature had surprised us with a pre-holiday snowfall outside. Snow is unusual in Louisiana, and Brandi called to say they were travelling around enjoying the scenery and wanted to stop over to see me. I knew by now that "they" included Dane and Jamie. If you've ever had your wisdom teeth extracted, you're familiar with the unpleasant taste inside your mouth and the overall awful sensation while you recuperate. But I didn't consider how I seemed.

They entered the living room and discovered me seated on the fireplace ledge. Dane and Brandi sat on the two-seater sofa, leaving three seats open for Jamie. Instead, he sat at my feet on the floor. It was strange, yet he seemed at ease there. We just laughed and grinned. They eventually left to enjoy the day.

The Mitchells were throwing another party. Momma was pleased to stay home with Maddie so I could go have some fun at the holiday festivities. She didn't have to make a second offer. I stepped into the party and noticed Jamie before he noticed me. I had butterflies in my stomach and thought, He somewhat likes me, and I could like him too. He was in the kitchen making another girl a drink. "Hey, Jamie,"

I said as I made my way to my friends. "Come over here and get us a drink," he said. We spent the rest of the night hanging out and flirting in a lighthearted manner. I recall thinking how great it was to be out, enjoying the attention of this successful, well-meaning man who was completely devoted to me. Jamie was entertaining and pleasant in the greatest way possible. We talked and laughed, and I couldn't help but think of Jamie and Casper's great contrasts. I had a crush on him.

Throughout the holidays, there were numerous gatherings that provided Jamie and me with opportunities to spend time together among groups of people. We swapped phone numbers and began messaging. We hadn't gone on a date yet, and the relaxed atmosphere we shared worked for me. Jamie appreciated me since Maddie was my top focus.

Brandi asked a large group of us to hang out at Dane's. I arrived with Maddie, and, of course, Jamie was present. We were all sitting on a big couch, and Maddie was playing at my feet. Jamie sat across from me in a relaxed setting. Maddie, who was usually clingy, warmed up to Jamie right away, and he adored her in return. Something about his demeanour spoke to me and, more crucially, to her. He exuded a silly confidence that made us feel at ease with him. Jamie was friendly and just a lovely guy in general.

We continued to spend a lot of time with our friends, but neither of us was ready to date. Our love sentiments, which we fought hard to suppress, came second to the bone Jamie, Maddie, and I shared. He was extremely patient, which added to his allure. Our slow burn relationship gave me time to get used to the concept of us. The more time I spent with my pals, the less wild insecure sentiments they instilled in me. I realised I wasn't insane or paranoid.

By the end of 2009, I was confident that my obligation to aid Casper's recovery was complete. Maddie and I have officially left the Liberty house. Casper was in a downward spiral for months, which had nothing to do with the accident and everything to do with the chemicals on which he had become reliant. All of my efforts to assist him were ignored, and the turbulence in our lives became intolerable. I debated what I should do to keep my daughter safe. Denying him visitation sounded extreme, but the uncertainty of the situation wasn't good for Maddie. Living at Momma's gave me the time I needed to figure out what was best for both of us. I was feeling better, like I was making progress in my and Maddie's lives. I began to let go of long-held grudges, hoping Casper would find a better path for himself. I wanted to support him in a way that didn't include me in his everyday challenges when I learned he was seeking professional therapy for his issues. Allowing him to stay in the Liberty House was the best option. I sold the Liberty house once he was in a better frame of mind and ready to go on.

7.

A Butterfly Gets Her Wings

It had been two years since I had announced to the world what I was expecting. I had cocooned myself during that period to nourish my now-thriving daughter. We had spent a little more than a year in Liberty, Mississippi, where I learned how to be the mother my daughter required. But I was determined that Maddie would not be held responsible for my faults merely because I was young. I needed to end the cycle of distrust, worry, and forgiveness. Casper's way of living undermined his capacity to be a good parent to our daughter. Casper's connection with Maddie began to deteriorate after we left Liberty. I tried to gather myself and move on with my life, but it was difficult for me. Panic crept in when I realised I was a single mother solely responsible for my daughter's well-being. I went through a tumultuous period of great sadness that left me listless and unmotivated. My world had shattered, but Maddie's was only getting started. Despite my dismay, her health and happiness flourished. The mother in me took over, and I focused all of my attention on being the best caregiver for my baby. I spent months introspectively processing the emotional turmoil of the prior years.

Learning to trust was the foundation of my transformation. I had to learn to trust not only my brain, but also my instincts. What appears to be healthy for us does not always feel right. I began to build criteria for trusting others and being secure in my judgments with the aid of family and good people in my life. The complications of being a child living as an adult heightened my anxiety to the point where I avoided making difficult decisions entirely. Maddie and I both suffered as a result of it. I also needed to accept responsibility for the breakdown of my relationship with Casper. Despite the fact that my inexperience and youth had worked against us, I learned that keeping him accountable for his actions, and thus my own, was critical. I'd only recently begun to realise who I was, and even at eighteen, I still had a long way to go before becoming a lady.

Being Maddie's mother and caring for her enriched my life and gave it new meaning. But on many days, she was the sole reason I got out of bed. I worked hard to keep my things together for her. The smile I used to wear for others had been replaced by one I exclusively wore for Maddie. We kept quiet for a while to avoid the press, and I devised a detailed timetable to ensure that all of Maddie's demands were addressed. I kept track of deadlines and knew when everything had to be completed. I was a self-diagnosed obsessive-compulsive at the time. I never considered it a disorder because its manifestations improved my life and Maddie's as well. She had no desires. I sang to her a lot, and we played a lot. Her happiness boosted mine. As I established my skill as a mother, my strength and confidence returned.

Joy slowly and steadily returned to my life. Jamie was a big part of that. The more time I spent with my friends, the happier I got. Jamie knew my attachment to Maddie and that we were a package deal. We had a deep and lasting friendship before our relationship blossomed into a romance.

Diane, Brandi, and I opted to stay home for a girls' night. Brandi recommended we go to Dane's family's house and relax in the pool and Jacuzzi. Dane and Jamie arrived somewhere in the early evening. Everyone eventually went home or to bed, but Jamie and I stayed up all night talking. I was amazed when the sun came up and we still hadn't run out of topics. I'd never remained awake all night with someone before. We didn't kiss or touch. But we were forming a friendship. My daddy's name is Jamie, and I recall chuckling at the concept. Jamie is my name, and now there's Jamie.

Jamie rapidly became an important part of my life. Jamie, Maddie, and I spent much of our time with friends, even as our sentiments increased, to ensure Maddie felt safe. We were usually a three-person team. We never wanted our growing affair to make her feel threatened. Jamie quickly put Maddie's needs ahead of his own and agreed she was the priority. We used to joke that he was only in the relationship for Maddie. The bond they shared was immediate. "Kismet" is the greatest term to describe him entering her life. Each of us learned to care for the other, and our friendship matured over time.

Brandi eventually insisted on the four of us going on a double date. Everything was new for Jamie and me, and I was looking forward to our first proper date. We drove to New Orleans to admire the Christmas decorations before stopping at a posh hotel for drinks. Brandi and I were sitting in the rear of the car on the way home. When I leaned in between the seats to change the radio station, Jamie kissed me. Oh, that's strange, I thought. But first, our first kiss. After that, he became increasingly interested in me. Casper, who felt my commitment was limitless, could sense me withdrawing in earnest now. I began scheduling appointments for him to see Maddie, always accompanied by one of his parents. Things were getting out of hand, and it wasn't the best moment to start dating. Jamie wanted to take me out, but I was afraid Casper would twist the truth and accuse me of wrongdoing. Jamie and I vowed to do everything possible to keep our relationship out of the press.

But the media picked up on the story and put a hideous photo of Jamie and another of me on the cover of Us Weekly. There were no photos of us together, and to be honest, we weren't serious at the time. Jamie and his mates laughed hysterically throughout the whole event. "Jamie," replied our friend Peter, who has since become the godfather of my second daughter Ivey. We've done some insane things throughout our lives. But you've really surpassed yourself this time." Jamie's sense of humour and genuineness were exactly what I needed to allow love to blossom between us. It wasn't lost on me that such a good man had been placed right in front of me after exiting a toxic relationship. I just couldn't open my heart that easily again. But as we spent more time together, his affection for Maddie grew. I was hesitant to introduce a man into our lives since I wasn't convinced he was the greatest fit for us at the time. Jamie's honesty and goodness were never in doubt; it was my own bad judgement and mistakes that kept me on alert. Our unconventional courting came and went several times during the first year and a half.

My artistic soul was also reawakening at this point. The sensation is similar to scratching an itch. I yearned to be able to create and express myself. My outlet of playing Zoey was no longer available, and I realised that portraying a character wouldn't provide me with what I needed at the time. I was filled with contradictory emotions that I wanted to communicate. Despite the fact that I'd spent years acting, music had always been a method for me to express myself.

Ms. Lou's questions from months ago returned to the forefront of my memory. It was time to start asserting my independence and making long-term plans for my professional future. Casper, I was confident, was incompetent and could not help us emotionally or financially in the long run. For a while, I had money from past employment and assumed Casper and I would share all of the parenting chores. But now the enormity of my financial duty as Maddie's sole provider hit me. I needed to do something to secure our future. The words "storytelling" and "music" sprang to mind.

Growing up in my house, there was always music playing around the clock. My mother's love of Elton John influenced me, while my father's love of country music created an interest in the genre. Women performers were producing power anthems and good songs when I was a kid. Shania Twain was a favourite of both my sister and myself, and I was a major admirer of the Chicks (originally the Dixie Chicks), Mariah Carey, Madonna, and Janet Jackson. All of their songs and experiences inspired my life, and I eventually chose to put my own ideas to music. Country music seemed like a natural fit for me. I admired pop music, but my songs were more in tune with my Southern heritage. The transition to songwriting felt effortless, but mastering my art was difficult.

Ms. Lou suggested I pay her a visit in Nashville, where I might explore my songwriting abilities and opportunities. I used one of her little offices to get away from the world and concentrate on putting my sentiments into words. I approached songwriting as if it were a profession. I stood up, went to the office, and began writing. I took advantage of the peaceful, introspective time to express myself. After demonstrating my writing talent and perseverance, I began to attend workshops with other writers and industry specialists. We'd sit in an office with our guitars and make music. These quick excursions to Nashville continued until I decided I needed to spend more time there if I wanted to keep developing my music. I needed to live and be visible in Music City if I was going to give this thing a fair go. I realised that if I wanted to be taken seriously as an artist and create great writing relationships, I needed to be available all the time. A move would also signify a new beginning for Maddie and myself. It would be my opportunity to demonstrate to my daughter that I was strong and capable, that I had the confidence to start from zero and establish a great future. Maddie's father was not going to stop us. He was dealing with his own troubles, and his trips to Maddie were sporadic. I was still okay with him having a relationship with her, but that wasn't going to keep me in Louisiana.

It was a scary decision for me to leave Louisiana. I was still figuring out how to be a mother. I grappled with my residual feelings from the previous years' decisions and sacrifices. My objective had been to offer a good life for Maddie, but the fact was that I was afraid of being alone, and as a result, we both paid the price. That anxiety kept me trapped in a loop of bad choices for myself and Maddie. Jamie knew I needed a change, and despite the fact that we'd be hours away, he understood my want to give it a shot. Jamie flew up to Nashville with us and assisted Maddie and me with our transition to our new home. During a period of enormous uncertainty, he remained supportive. He believed in me, and that faith provided me with support throughout my life. I paused our love relationship. It didn't make sense to try to make a new relationship work while starting a new job, moving to a new place, and caring for a young child.

Brandi had recently finished nursing school, and I invited her to come to Nashville to assist me with Maddie. I thought it was a fantastic chance for both of us, but she chose to remain in Louisiana and start a family with Dane. Instead, I hired Erin, who was fantastic. Soon after I called it quits with Jamie, Erin called to tell me that dozens of roses had been delivered to me and Maddie. Jamie and I were both hurt by the break, and a new type of friendship developed. We opted not to make a decision. We kept in touch and saw one other on a regular basis.

Nashville's daily existence was the best kind of hectic. We lived in a lovely mansion in the Governors Club, and I was completely dedicated to Maddie and music. Maddie's days were filled, and Momma came by frequently to assist with her care. I soaked up musical information like a sponge. I took guitar classes and learned scales and chords, as well as the Nashville Number System, which is a mechanism for understanding chord progression. It facilitates playing by ear. I wanted to understand the subtleties of studio recording and working with musicians. For example, I was curious about the phrase "on the two" and how chords were converted into numbers. It's like learning a completely new language. I practised the guitar till my calluses formed and I mastered the number system. Being a part of that musical community restored professional meaning to my life.

In many ways, the move was a positive adjustment for us, and starting over motivated me in all facets of my life. I resolved to push myself and study for the ACT. With so many good institutions in Nashville, I thought college was a definite option. I had studied for months and was convinced that I would do well on the exam. Momma and Maddie dropped me off at the local high school where the exam was administered on the day of the exam. It was an odd experience. I entered the room, pencils in hand, and sat at one of the desks. Despite the fact that there was only a year or two between myself and the other exam takers, I felt out of place. Several folks turned around and stared within minutes. I could hear the whispering. "Does that look like Jamie Lynn Spears?""Are we on a reality show?"" "Isn't that her?" "What exactly is she doing here?"" It was a strange sensation. The proctor soon arrived, and the focus shifted to the exam. When the findings arrived, I ripped the envelope open with childlike glee. My score demonstrated that I was capable of getting into a good school. I considered a full-time college experience while managing Maddie and a blossoming music career, but I couldn't see myself being able to accomplish it all. Maddie and music were my passions, so I pursued both. I believed in the value of education, but I also had a child to care for and bills to pay.

For a few months, Jamie and I maintained our version of a long-distance romance, but the demands of parenthood and working in Tennessee proved too much for me to handle. I cut it off. Jamie remained a close friend, and I knew that no matter what happened in the future, he would always be a part of our life.

My assistant Erin needed to move on, so I hired my buddy Kayla, who had recently gotten out of a bad business deal. I appreciated having a friend I could rely on to be there for me and Maddie. She was also friendly with Jamie, and she kept me updated on his whereabouts.

Maddie and I would go to Momma's house in Kentwood on weekends so Casper could stay in Maddie's life. Casper stated that he was attempting to break free from his destructive habits and had sought expert assistance. Nonetheless, given his previous gaffes and unreliability, I found it difficult to leave her with him. We agreed to supervised visits closer to where he lived in Mississippi at this point. Casper gradually demonstrated to me that he was ready to resume a good relationship with our daughter. I was so desperate for Maddie to be close to her father that I overlooked the warning signs. We went to Louisiana for the holidays, and Casper played the role of father, lavishing us both with care. He wanted to pay us a visit in Nashville, and I didn't see why not. Casper arrived enthusiastically and spent precious time with Maddie. He was helpful to Maddie and behaving like the parent she deserved. We went to the park and shared lunch. Maddie appeared to be content. At first, I saw how being a family would benefit all of us. But Casper and I didn't have a genuine connection. In fact, I felt excluded, if not self-conscious, around him. Despite this, I kept thinking to myself, Maddie deserves a family. After the first trip to Nashville, he persuaded me to return and, eventually, to give us another shot. I was once again duped into believing that we could make this work for our little girl. He moved in with us, and I soon began to have the same old doubts. Casper gradually exposed his actual self. He was hesitant to look for work and made excuses for not being able to find work. He started undermining my newly found confidence almost immediately. Casper would instruct me how to do things and would critique how I did them. Everything was paid for, and his petty reasons for not getting a job remained.

Jamie and I communicated on a regular basis, and I owed him a phone call to inform him that Casper had returned to my life. I'd been putting off telling Jamie since I knew he'd be disappointed. The thought of disappointing him sickened me. I knew I had to inform him at some point. I couldn't reach him on the phone, so I texted him. It started out well enough, but the moment I told him the news, the tone of his comments shifted in a way I'd never seen before. Jamie's opinion was really important to me. Every syllable was tinged with rage and disappointment. "Are you aware of the error you're making for yourself and Maddie?" He's garbage. He's proven it numerous times. He is untrustworthy. Being with him is awful, Jamie Lynn! He's trash, and being with him makes you trash as well. It causes me to doubt what I know about you."

I was hurt, and his judgments harmed me a lot. Jamie had never been so severe before, but that was exactly what I needed to hear. It only took a few weeks for me to understand that Casper was up to his old tricks again. I eventually saw through his parasitic nature and recognized how horrible he was for us. The atmosphere in the house was tight. I became nervous, but Jamie's remarks gave me the courage to put an end to things for good. Casper stated that he was heading home for a brief stay. I resolved to have "the breakup talk" when he returned. But after a few days, I realised something was amiss. Casper did not answer the phone when I called, and he never contacted me again. I spotted a post on a girl's social media page that I followed, and there he was. Casper had returned to Mississippi and reverted to his destructive ways. I didn't have to wonder what had happened anymore. More photos and reports about him cheating on me followed. Casper's leaving comforted me, but the lingering humiliation sealed the end of our relationship.

I knew I'd have to do something radical to get rid of Casper. For years, I'd concealed behind a false grin, convincing everyone that everything was fine. Now I had to tell my family that nothing was as it seemed. I called Momma and told her, "Casper is gone—and he's never coming back." She listened as I detailed some of the cunning and twisted ways Casper had exploited me, how I had enabled behaviours that put us in danger to go unchecked. I admitted that I had battled every warning sign in my thoughts for months in order to keep us together for Maddie. Momma told me that she didn't realise Casper had become completely untrustworthy until recently. Maddie,

Kayla, and I joined Britney on her Femme Fatale Tour after she summoned the Spears army. I spent the time telling her about the terrible details of my life and loneliness. Daddy, who had stepped up to assist Britney throughout her troubles in recent years, was also on the tour. He assisted in removing the extortionists and conspirators from her life and had even pledged his sobriety in support of Britney. The conservatorship was only a small part of his dedication to assisting her. They remained sober together, and witnessing my father prioritise Britney's needs over his own helped my old resentments recede. For a time, the conservatorship required Britney to be drug and alcohol tested on a regular basis. In solidarity, my father offered to do it with her. This was the first time in my life that someone held them accountable for their actions, and the constant anxiety that I had lived with for so long suddenly dissipated. I could relax about their sobriety.

We began to spend time together in order to mend our broken relationship. He apologised to me for causing me years of humiliation and embarrassment. "Jamie Lynn," he said. I know I don't deserve to be in your or your child's life. But I'm hoping you'll let me earn your trust again." Getting over my previous two years' experiences helped me see Daddy was doing his best to do the right thing, and for that alone, I gradually welcomed him back into my life. I did not simply forgive and forget. There were some restrictions, such as no drinking and only engaging in healthful behaviours. Daddy usually keeps his half of the bargain, unless he doesn't and I have to kick him out of my life for a bit.

Travelling with my sister and the folks we considered family was the best medication. On that tour, I took the first steps toward being the woman I wanted to be. It took some time for me to stop chastising myself and start thinking more positively, but somewhere along the way I recognized I'd done everything I could to make it work with Casper, and that simple realisation made going ahead easier.

I returned to Nashville with a renewed sense of purpose. Jamie was relieved to hear Casper was gone, but she wondered if I would make the same mistake again. "Nope, this time it's game over," I said, and our friendship was restored, and I returned to my life in Nashville. Jamie dated another woman, and acquaintances introduced me to men they thought were "perfect" for me. They were frequently professional athletes, and the dates were always fun, but their celebrity didn't provide us with the connection my friends expected. One night, a guy I had a couple dates with called. When I questioned what he was doing, he answered, "I'm out with a friend," which turned out to be another guy I had been out with. Only in my wacky life, I thought. I immediately discovered that going out and being seen by the public did not excite me in the least. I was consumed by parenthood, writing, and singing.

Ms. Lou suggested that I see a therapist to help me sort through the trauma of the last few years and my persistent anxieties. I wasn't totally sold on the concept and thought I understood my depression spells. In the past, I'd experienced spells of sadness and disillusionment that manifested in many ways. I attributed these bouts to hormonal changes and the stress of everything I had been through. Until I saw some of my sister's difficulties, I assumed that most of it was just part of growing up. I was only eighteen at the time, and I had no idea how serious the situation was. Some days, getting out of bed was virtually impossible. During other times of stress, I'd entirely lose my appetite and my weight would plummet. Although talking with someone seemed to help, the cycle would inevitably resurface. I did my best to cope and discovered that my creative outlet was a powerful remedy to my emotional issues. Aside from the joys of parenthood, I'd always struggled to maintain a genuine degree of pleasure. Looking back, I believe I spent so much time trying to be what everyone else required that I never discovered what truly satisfied myself. That discovery would be made a few years later.

Work restored balance to my life. Living in Nashville proved to be a valuable asset to my burgeoning music career. Anyone who met me could see my dedication. I spent a lot of time with musicians and other writers. I discovered that there were various methods to songwriting. I went to composing rooms, where two or more musicians collaborated for hours on end. I had the opportunity to collaborate with various songwriters, including Chris Tompkins. I've met hundreds of renowned people in my life, but I've never been starstruck as I did when I met talented composers like Chris. Meeting the man responsible for some of the best songs ever recorded was uplifting and left me dumbfounded. Chris has written songs for Carrie Underwood, Martina McBride, and Luke Bryan, among others. I could cover a full page with his impressive résumé, which includes "Before He Cheats," "Blown Away," and "Drunk on You." But, like many others, Chris put me at ease almost quickly. He sat down with a guitar and requested that I tell him a story. He'd pluck a few chords, then take my words and turn them into magic. He informed me that my experience was worth telling, just as it was for everyone eager to share theirs. "If it happened, you can tell it." My life's soundtrack was my history. I spent months expressing aspects of myself and creating music that revealed my most vulnerable sides.

I also collaborated with Liz Rose, one of country music's most renowned and celebrated songwriters. She'd written hit songs for Taylor Swift, Miranda Lambert, and Carrie Underwood, among others. She had received an Academy of Country Music award and had been nominated for several Grammys. I was honoured and humbled that she saw potential in me and wanted to collaborate with me. Liz was educated, and the experience was inspiring. She was fantastic to work with and encouraged me to keep going when I became discouraged. I didn't realise how certain songs could come to me in minutes and others would force me on a journey of great self-discovery and emotional hardship until I started writing. Making music is all about me-the raw, blemished, and imperfect me. My audience hear the finished song but are unaware of the motivation or the hours spent creating and recording it. Once a song is released, it is open to interpretation by others. My song becomes theirs, and if my vision gets lost along the road, well, that's a natural result of sharing music with the rest of the world. Music takes us all to another place and time. It elicits memories and feelings like no other media.

When I wasn't caring for Maddie (nurturing, having playdates, or attending to her needs), I was writing and performing. Like other Nashville musicians, I started out by doing small-venue shows. I took my music to a few labels, who told me I should keep going, which I did. I continued to write and perform. I sang in a number of Broadway's honky-tonks and bars.

Maddie and I visited family in Louisiana in between concerts. Maddie and her father's visits became less frequent month after month. Casper's struggles with drugs and alcohol, as well as his run-ins with the law, are well documented. He was unable to pay child support. His interest in her began to diminish. The father-daughter link was fraying, and I felt driven to do everything possible to safeguard my daughter. I went to family court several times to protect Maddie's interests and was eventually granted full custody. I continued to encourage Maddie and her father to have supervised visits. Before spending time with his daughter, the judge ordered that he be drug tested. He objected to the idea and, at times, did not bother to come. His parents wanted to keep a good relationship with Maddie, but their son was always first. I began to doubt their ability to prioritise Maddie's safety, and the relationship continued to deteriorate over time. I was committed to give Maddie opportunities to visit her father, but only if everyone followed the court-mandated rules.

The pandemonium at home wasn't going to undo all of my hard work in the studio. I'd spent the previous few years honing my songwriting skills. I met a lot of musicians and opted to collaborate with a producer who put together a great band for me. I was pleased with the music and began to perform it live. I was initially hesitant to expose my soul to the world night after night. Each song transports me to a different moment and location in my life, leaving me feeling raw and exposed at times. As the weeks went, revisions were made to the plans, and I simply accepted them. They were still my tunes, but something didn't feel right. Music experts who I believed understood me began to influence my approach and how I handled myself onstage. I had a great deal of respect and appreciation for the guidance I received from everyone around me. I might have been able to consent to these modifications earlier in my career. But I'd changed my mind about how I wanted to show myself, and I couldn't be what they envisioned. I started to feel like a puppet or like I was at a country music star summer camp. Nothing felt quite right. My annoyance mounted, and I became very robotic in my response to my surroundings. I felt like a product, rather than myself—a doll made to look the part. It left me hollow and uneasy. I couldn't reconcile their creation with the highly individualistic nature of my music. Nothing felt genuine to me. Was I insufficient?

I began to mistrust myself, which resulted in an increase in worry. I felt adrift and lost control of my own actions once more. My investment of time and money in the production was not generating the desired results. More significantly, I felt suffocated and uneasy in my own skin. This all came to a head when a concert was planned for a limited group of industry insiders, fans, and invited guests. Originally, I was assured that the venue would be packed with many of my supporters, both domestic and international. Nothing beats walking out onstage in front of a cheering crowd. But I was already feeling vulnerable at the time, and as I approached the microphone, the lack of good energy in the room disarmed me. I had the impression that the audience was expecting to be wowed. The strain was intense, but I was trained to persevere and give my all in these situations. My band and I began our first song. To get through it, I had to be hyper-focused, when previously, performance was automatic and fluid. The audience warmed up a little, but I was unravelling internally. Something was going on. The words and timing faded like smoke rising into the air as the music for the third song began. I was able to improvise my way through the performance. However, for the first time, I raced through the song's conclusion. The expectations placed on me as a young performer had always pushed me to do my absolute best in all I did. I'm Spears, and nothing less than flawless will do. That pressure, which had previously served me well, began to weaken my confidence and abilities. I was terrified. When I reflected on what went wrong after the presentation, I convinced myself that the appearance had been badly organised and had not met my expectations.

Unfortunately, the panic got more with each passing day. The breaking point occurred during a practice session in the studio with the band. My father and the producers were present while we ran through the songs. The stress of having Dad in the room may have exacerbated my already existing anxiousness. I was always striving to be the greatest at anything I did. The session should have been simple, even enjoyable. But I was too focused on myself, second-guessing what seemed right. Here I was, singing my own words and telling my own stories in an awkward way. A quick and intense sensation overtook me as I was singing and aware that I was being examined. I experienced acute stage fear like I'd never experienced before. I'd never had anything like it before. The closest I came was the intense self-consciousness I had in high school whenever I played sports, whenever I entered the field or stepped onto the court. I resembled a human lightning rod. I didn't want to be the centre of attention or be mocked for my performance, so I became a cheerleader. This was unique. My brain felt like it was turning dark, like everything was shutting down. The dread of the moment materialised physically, and I grasped a table, afraid I'd pass out. I sat down on a couch, and Dad joined me. I was still dizzy and couldn't recall having eaten anything that day.

My father looked me in the eyes and said, "Jamie Lynn, you should go home and get things right." I knew he was right. I needed to take things slowly. I was desperate to return to Louisiana as quickly as possible. I quickly realized that a strong, bold woman realizes when she is in over her head.

8.

Much More Than the Right Guy

I left the studio, made a few phone calls, and packed only what Maddie and I needed. I was generally very organised and efficient, but my lack of focus was really a symptom of a much larger problem. Tickets were ordered in advance. We were on our way to the airport, looking forward to seeing family, friends, and familiar faces. I knew instinctively that the comfort and security of home would bring the much-needed relaxation. My mother would be there to help with Maddie and give me the time I needed to recover from my anguish and agitation.

I had a chance to collect my hurried thoughts on the aircraft ride home and try to figure out where everything went wrong. Maybe it was my upbringing or my experiences in the entertainment industry. The descent into disillusionment began with my apprehension about changing so many facets of my performance. I went to Nashville with a plan and a good feeling about where I was going. My songwriting gave me the opportunity to connect with my innermost ideas and reveal myself in a completely different way. I was naked and vulnerable, and I was free to be myself. But it felt terrible when people began to cover me with production, presentation, and style adjustments. Every idea I had about myself was opposed by their ideas. None of this was beneficial to my mental health. I desired control and the ability to set my own path.

One of my initial thoughts was to contact Jamie. We'd spent the previous few months conversing frequently, and I knew he'd be there for me. He has always provided me with solace. Jamie could tell something was wrong the moment he took up the phone. Jamie was incredible to me; he gave levity and comedy to the weight of my position by saying things like, "Jamie Lynn, yeah, you're nuts—but all the good ones are." And guess what? That's OK." He never made me feel uncomfortable, and his comprehension made me feel normal.

While I was home, I remained at Momma's. Within a few days, I realised I needed professional assistance. I was no stranger to worry and fear, but my previously learned coping techniques were no longer effective. Unlike the Nashville sessions, I realised I needed to be invested in the process if I was going to get through this. In all honesty, I basically told other doctors what I felt they wanted to hear. Previously, a counsellor would ask questions and affirm my tepid responses. I wasn't willing to delve deep and confront the issues that were robbing me of happiness. For years, I thought I was doing well, and I was still caught up in the pattern of pretending everything was alright. But what happened in Nashville terrified me, as did some of my sister's actions. I didn't want to fall into a hole from which I wouldn't be able to recover. I sought the advice and expertise of a professional in whom I had faith. I found a new psychologist in Louisiana with whom I felt comfortable expressing difficult and personal elements of my life that I had never previously communicated. This time felt different since I had my family and Jamie by my side. I was now ready to open up and address the source of my problems. My anxiety, sadness, and obsessive-compulsive disorder were all officially diagnosed. I had done well up to that point. But the convergence of everything-pregnancy, public humiliation, stress, a failed romance, and so on-was too much for me to bear. It required a lot of effort on my part to keep it all together. I committed to regular appointments and rapidly felt the benefits of being at home and receiving professional therapy. I knew I was on the correct track. My plan was to rest for a few weeks before returning to Nashville, refreshed and ready to record. Then, in the shape of a broken bone, life gave me a curveball.

One thing that drove me insane about Momma's place was the lack of a strong Wi-Fi signal. I had some emails to follow up on one day and knew the only way I was going to get a good signal was to step outside to the second-floor balcony outside the bedroom. I walked out the door, and it was too late when I realised the door automatically shut when closed. Anyone who has lived in that property can tell you about the balcony door. I wasn't worried at first because the balcony had a glass wall that overlooked the living room, where Momma and Maddie were playing. When I finished my work, I looked through the glass and saw that the living room was empty. I made an impulsive decision to climb over the balustrade to a lower wall and leap down. My plan's physics failed, and I jumped twenty feet, breaking a bone in my heel. My life was altered by that fracture.

After I went to the ER and had X-rays, the doctor ordered a boot for my broken heel, and I was out of commission for several weeks. Naturally, this restricted my movement and driving habits. Momma was quite helpful to Maddie. I was obliged to take it easy for a while, and aside from attending therapy appointments and the occasional outing, I spent the majority of my time recovering from my injuries. My days were spent on the couch, and Jamie spent all of his spare time with me. Apart from my daughter, the only thing that felt nice was being with him. He was a healer. Jamie would bring me food and, more importantly, companionship. We used that time to get to know one other on a more personal level. I eventually allowed him to get to know me. When he stated it was all he ever wanted, he meant it. He would bring movies most days. Jamie introduced me to old and renowned films. He insisted on watching all of The Godfather films with us. He'd start the movie, and we'd be deep in conversation within a few minutes. Something would spark a discussion, and the movie would soon be forgotten. There was also the occasional sleep. I have yet to watch them in their entirety to this day. Jamie made sure I laughed a lot and didn't take my problems too seriously. To keep Maddie entertained, he drove me to my doctor's appointments and took her out for ice cream. It was odd that he'd keep Maddie busy with treats while I was attempting to keep my world from collapsing. He and I were still figuring out who we were to each other, and his willingness to walk that path with me and Maddie seemed shockingly meaningful.

My therapy meetings were critical in assisting me in transitioning into a healthier phase of my life. Getting in touch with the proper therapist made all the difference. My psychologist suggested that I try medication to alleviate my symptoms while we worked through the underlying causes of my problems. The medications did more harm than good, leaving me weary and indifferent, making day-to-day life difficult. I could hardly get out of bed at times because I was exhausted. I stayed on medication for months at my doctor's recommendation, and much to my dismay, it did not solve my problems and made others worse. The most successful treatment was talking about the anxiety, and medication support, while effective for many, did not work for me. Talking openly about my anxiety made it easier for me to articulate my needs and desires. I had only recently discovered how liberating it was to speak my truth and my hardships. Recognizing that I was unhappy with my job situation was the first step toward making drastic adjustments in my life. Sharing my ideas with Jamie helped to validate the ideals I had for my profession.

Jamie's genuine concern and support for my well-being was the catalyst that expanded my affection for him over time. His unwavering devotion for me—just Jamie Lynn, not the performer or celebrity—healed a part of me that neither medicine nor therapy could. He taught me that simply being myself was sufficient. That lesson stayed with me and permeated every element of my life. I began to consider how I wanted to live and what would make me happy. Jamie and Maddie's quick connection got deeper as we spent more time together. Jamie was completely devoted to both of us. I suppose I fell in love with him more because of his feelings for Maddie. He added that being the type of mother I was made him love me even more. Although our connection was not love at first sight, I believe it was parenting at first sight.

Jamie laughs that he had no idea who I was when we first met. He obviously recognized my surname but knew nothing else about me. That gave me some solace. Jamie is ten years my senior, so it would have been strange if he was watching Zoey 101 or following my career. Jamie's appearance in our lives felt fortuitous. He saw my artistic nature and encouraged my profession. He recently told me that when he first met me, he thought I was the most gorgeous female he'd ever seen and asked, "Why would she ever want to be with me?"

After a few weeks at home, I decided to return to Nashville and continue making music in the way that seems real to me. We stayed close and bridged the gap with weekend visits and phone chats. But after a while, none of us felt that was enough. I had transformed into we. We desired a more stable life for Maddie, one in which she could be surrounded by relatives and form long-lasting friendships. Jamie and I wanted to be in the same city so that we could focus on our romance. Louisiana was beckoning me back. But first, I needed to finish some work.

My self-discovery journey in Tennessee concluded in my reclaiming my authority and doing things on my own terms. I moved back to Nashville and let the majority of the production team go. We were all aware that it wasn't functioning. Everyone acknowledged I had the gift, and I was determined to use it as authentically as possible. The therapy process taught me more about how to succeed in the field. I needed to be a part of the decision-making process and have control over the trajectory of my career. Only with that level of control would I be able to pursue the job I want. I'd been sculpted, directed, moulded, and controlled for years. I'd had to do what my bosses and parents demanded. If it wasn't my own team making the decisions, it was the studio. I was shutting down when people tried to take control of my life now that I was no longer a child star. NO MORE, I resolved. For the first time, I was prepared to take control of my content and brand.

I dialled Liz Rose's number and spoke with her for a long time, as her musical knowledge transcended everyone I knew at the time. But my regard for Liz extends beyond the professional. Liz was a mentor who shielded me from others, but especially from myself. When sessions didn't feel right, she stepped in. Liz's strong résumé made it easy for her to make suggestions or revisions. She had great faith in my composition and singing abilities and encouraged me to keep developing the format for presenting my music to the rest of the world. Selling my music to labels led me down the wrong path, one that compromised my independence. Liz and Corey Crowder, a very brilliant producer and writer, provided the framework for my musical path. We talked about where I saw myself in the country music business and how to get my music out to the public multiple times. They offered a thorough instruction on the many methods for releasing music. The music industry was still reeling from the arrival of music streaming services. Artists were using the internet to grow their fan bases, and streaming services gave them a new venue to share their music. Musicians, like authors who self-publish books, suddenly have different methods of releasing music. I had faith that Corey and Liz would be able to provide the knowledge and skill required to make my album in a way that was distinct from what the large businesses offered. Liz, who lived in Dallas, suggested I visit for a writing retreat. Our creative circle was completed by Lisa Carver, whose songs have been performed by legends such as Tim McGraw, Reba McEntire, and Sugarland. We talked for days, shared tales, and wrote the majority of the music for my 2014 EP.

We devised and implemented a strategy. I spent months writing a song that captured what Jamie and I had gone through on our journey to love. We encountered various difficulties along the road. After overcoming everything I had to overcome in order to open myself up to love, fear, humiliation, self-doubt, and trust, the song I wrote expressed my journey in a manner I hadn't been able to express before. Early on, I published my tune "How Could I Want More," which is about being with someone who appears to be great for you but fighting with the inner anguish that there may be something more. The song's final phrase was originally "He ought to be the right guy." Jamie and I were engaged by the time I recorded the song for my EP in 2014. And the final phrase was appropriately modified to "I know he is the right guy."

Jamie was working on a plan at the same time. Jamie planned to propose with the support of Momma and my pals. He had planned an extravagant day for the three of us. He ordered us to be ready by ten o'clock in the morning. Maddie and I dressed up for a day of fun with Jamie. I believed we were going to the IMAX to see a movie, but after a few minutes I realised we were going somewhere else. Jamie knows how much I enjoy Louisiana history and architecture, so he took us to one of my favourite locations. We spent hours investigating the grandeur of the structure, nature, and stories of Oak Alley. The canopy of oak trees that genuinely transforms the land sets the tone for a magnificent day. The enormous trees gave cover and shade from the scorching March sun. Jamie and I read about the history of the landmark while sharing secret smiles and hushed discussions. Something about the day felt distinct, even unique to me. Maddie just wanted to spend the day with us, holding our hands or sprinting ahead on the expansive grounds. Jamie insisted on driving to New Orleans and taking a walk along the river after we ended our stay. I almost stumbled, exhausted from my hours at Oak Alley. But he appeared so eager to go that I couldn't say no. He parked the car, and the three of us went for a walk down the Riverwalk. As we walked, we didn't say much. Maddie was distracted by the crowds around her. He got down on one knee before I realised what was going on. Uh, what is he doing? I wondered. He pulled out a ring and asked, "Will you marry me?" without any prelude. "Will you let me marry you and your momma?"

he asked, pulling out another ring. "Yeah!" she said, and so did I. He put the ring on my finger, which was somewhat larger than Maddie's. We took some alone time to appreciate the moment. Jamie had a photographer on hand to document everything. Just as my disbelief was wearing off, he began to urge us along, saying something like, "Come on, we've got to leave. Everyone is patient." What? I wondered yet again. "Waiting for what?" I inquired. Jamie had arranged for the crucial people in our lives to meet at a nearby friend's apartment. When we stepped in, our entire family and close friends were there to celebrate and salute us with champagne. But there was more to it. Momma was taking Maddie home with her, and Jamie and I were going out to supper and drinks with friends. Jamie, knowing I'd been out all day, had Kayla come with new clothing and hair and cosmetics supplies. It was a fantastic evening. Jamie prepared every detail, and the day was wonderfully magical, just as I had anticipated.

Maddie, Jamie, and I fell in love. Our love is founded on mutual respect and regard for one another. We have a direct honesty that keeps us safe and allows no place for insecurities or doubts. We've found our footing as a couple, and I've finally found the security I've been looking for after years of juggling my identities as a celebrity, a Southern girl, and a mother. There are moments when my development is hampered by anxiousness. I told Jamie I was nervous and wanted to postpone our wedding just a few weeks into our engagement. "I am not calling everyone to tell them that!" he simply rolled his eyes. He simply listened and assisted me in rationalising my worry. He was so confident in our connection that he was able to simply reassure me.

I had never known pure happiness until this time. I am neither foolish nor naive. My work life has been filled with accomplishments and recognition. Those achievements gave me happiness and pleasure. But pure enjoyment is a relatively new phenomenon for me. As I look at my professional background, full of money and celebrity, I realise that none of it produced the satisfaction I discovered once I had the courage to make sensible decisions based on my intuition and delight. After Maddie, I was finally able to focus on my personal needs rather than those of my extended family, team, or career. It was a great accomplishment for me to release my songs independently. Moving back home seemed as natural as breathing. My focus shifted to returning to Louisiana and creating a life I actually valued. Jamie, Maddie, and I formed a family. I was at ease working remotely since I had done it before, and I was also confident in handling both the personal and business elements of my life.

2014 was a significant year for me. I launched my EP, The Journey, after years of trial and error, learning, observing, and writing. I felt a strong sense of success and pride in the music I was sharing with the rest of the world. It's a highly personal album in which each song represents a bit of myself-my experiences and feelings blended with a soulful country vibe. It's the soundtrack to my adolescence. For the first time, the music reflected me rather than the roles I played. It was both horrifying and thrilling at the same time. In order to promote the album, I needed to go on the road and perform, which included a lengthy radio tour. The music industry is complicated; it is not like television or movies. You must get in front of the correct people-radio station program directors. Typically, these PDs are given a prearranged list of performers by executives who have deals with major companies to play their musicians. Music is an enormous business. It's why you hear the same thirty songs over and over on a modern pop or country music station. However, by performing in front of crowds and meeting program directors across the country, independent artists have a better opportunity of gaining the attention of radio executives. Appearances on radio shows and conversations with influential DJs can also help a band's appeal.

So, after embarking on a lengthy tour, I took an extended weekend vacation in March 2014 to marry. Jamie had proposed marriage about a year before. Jamie and I chose to marry before the tour because of the upcoming release of my album and the travel that would be required in support of the music. It seemed only natural that Maddie would take part as a "mini bride." On a gorgeous spring day, the ceremony took place at the Audubon Tea Room and Sea Lion Colonnade. It was a lovely occasion made much more special by the fact that the wedding party consisted entirely of our nieces and nephews. As we exchanged vows, the adults sat with the invited guests. The gathering was filled with love and laughter. When we were exchanging vows, some photographers crept in and attempted to photograph our private moment. Security personnel quickly tackled them to the ground and escorted them out. Jamie and I had no idea it had happened until others told us later in the evening.

Within hours of saying "We do," I was packing and heading out on the road with my band. Jamie stayed behind to run his own company and care for Maddie. I would try to return home as much as possible, or they would come to wherever I was for the weekend. Maddie had become my entire universe from the day she was born. Nothing and no one had come before her. My own childhood memories of being forced to travel, the instability, and being left behind were still vivid. I never wanted Maddie to feel like she was being overlooked or overlooked because of my work. Jamie and I collaborated to reassure Maddie that she would remain our first focus. She was just six years old at the time, but she was wise and foresaw the changes that restarting my career would bring. She had complete faith in me. Maddie's youthful enthusiasm was contagious and influenced my decision to do the radio tour. Jamie and Maddie's close bond eased my concerns about leaving. I knew that our extended relatives in Louisiana would be there for them if they needed anything.

Life on the road was difficult. I missed my family and the

predictability of home. There was no place to cook or eat nutritious foods. It was a free-for-all with junk food. I liked the saturated fat and mysterious ingredients of fast food to my early pregnancy meals of Wheat Thins with cream cheese and pepper jelly. Being on the road, like filming, limits your freedom and space. I was sitting around a lot in preparation for the next interview or show. I was enthusiastic about the music, and nothing beats performing in front of a live crowd, feeling their enthusiasm and receiving an immediate reaction. It was even more exciting when someone shouted, "Hey, Zoey!" or "We love you, Jamie Lynn!" The silence that occurs immediately before I begin, when the audience calms down and ready for me to sing, is unlike any other. The world comes to a halt, and everyone waits for me to begin. It's fascinating. Nonetheless, the devotion of thousands of admirers pales in comparison to the actual love and respect that awaited me at home. I understood how fickle fans can be, and I realised that nothing could feed my spirit on a daily basis the way my daughter and husband could. Jamie and Maddie were supportive of my work and understood the importance of promoting my music and realising my ambition. Jamie understood my career objectives and appreciated that I had arrived at this point on my own terms. I needed to finish it. The time I spent travelling tested my life vision and priorities. Maddie and Jamie did good without me, and I did fine without them. But "fine" and "manage" aren't enough. We were a newlywed family, and I was looking forward to seeing everyone again. After the tour, I continued to promote my music while staying as close to home as feasible. That's where I learned we flourished. Since the release of my EP, I've had numerous offers to perform at various places. I've performed at the Ryman Auditorium as well as the Grand Ole Opry. My experiences there, singing in those venues, brought a long-awaited dream to fruition. On one specific occasion, I had just exited the stage, where my father was standing. We were laughing and enjoying the moment when a country music legend approached us. I looked up, my smile almost painfully big. I'm sure it appeared to be that way. "Hello,

Jamie Lynn," the man said. You were fantastic out there." I believe I whispered a thank you. We snapped a short photo together. I was trembling with excitement as Garth moved away to take the stage. As we approached the exit, I grasped Daddy's arm. "Oh my God, Daddy, Garth Brooks." By the time the exit door closed behind us, we realised we'd passed up an opportunity to see him play from the stage. Later, I emailed Maddie the photo of us with Garth Brooks, and she, being a great Food Network fan, asked, "Momma, isn't that Trisha Yearwood's husband?" "Did you get a picture of her as well?"

This was around the time Maddie began to inquire about my pregnancy. I knew Jamie was in favour of growing our family, but I needed to take care of business and get my career on track first. I begged Maddie, "Just give me a little time, Maddie." Fortunately, Jamie remained supportive and never made me feel awful for wanting to delay adding another member to the family for a little longer.

9.

The Sacrifice for Stardom

Hollywood's glamour isn't what it appears to be. Being a child performer is similar to being a student athlete in that there is always a sacrifice, a part of yourself that you give up to achieve the goal. Without a doubt, I aspired to be an actor and performer. I've loved playing roles since I was a little girl, and I've loved the reactions I've had from entertaining everyone who will watch. My parents were not the driving force behind my success, but they emphasised that if I wanted to act, I would devote my entire life to honing my craft. Because my elder sister was a pop icon and cameras were always present, I was exposed to people in positions of power in the industry. But just because a production assistant saw my potential doesn't mean I didn't work hard to be the best at what I performed on-screen.

As a young woman starting out in Hollywood, I had no idea what I was getting myself into-and I suspect many of my contemporaries would agree. The entertainment industry and its executives follow a different set of norms. It was and still is a predominantly male-dominated hierarchy with the ability to make or break any career.

Getting a job on television is one of the most exhilarating experiences anyone can have. It is undeniably unusual, comparable to winning the Powerball lottery. However, many individuals are unaware of the dedication, work, and sacrifice required to reach such a goal. When I first learnt to speak, I began acting. When my parents realised I had talent, they made sure I worked hard to improve. I took voice and dancing lessons in Baton Rouge, which was 45 minutes away. I took headshots and attended numerous auditions. I auditioned for and acted in several local plays and musicals. My siblings felt the same way, whether it was sports or the arts. I believe there is a widespread misperception that if you are born with skill, you will find success and glory. I can promise you that all of the young women that came up with me in the 1990s were completely committed to furthering their careers.

However, obtaining ambition necessitates the loss of autonomy. I can only speak for myself; everyone's path to success may be unique, but there are many common stops along the way. I dreamed of performing and bringing characters to life as a child. When I was old enough to realise that I could be on television and make money, I was like, "Sign me up." But it didn't occur to me at the age of eight that I would have to give up anything. I lacked the maturity and foresight to understand what I would have to give up in order to advance my profession. Later on, I would realise that I had been forced to give up control and my personality. My life stopped being mine the moment I entered the entertainment industry. I didn't realise it at first since I was so engrossed in fulfilling my dream. To be entirely honest, I was shielded from most of the tactics placed on actresses throughout my time there. There were a lot of dos and don'ts by the time I signed up for Zoey 101. Contracts have clauses that make a slew of demands, and stipulations are typically woven throughout every deal. The agreements can vary from project to project and from person to person. It's not as intrusive as it was fifty years ago, when studios would force you to date a costar for promotional purposes. Nowadays, it is largely about appearances, promotion, and information flow. Agreements may include phrases such as "do not change your appearance," "avoid negative press," and "termination clauses" for various types of transgressions. As a child raised with a firm hand, I was used to following rules. I didn't have the luxury of time or the ability to do what I wanted, when I wanted. I wasn't very interested in the Hollywood way of life. Maybe it had something to do with Britney's problems with the media, or maybe it was because I'd started seeing Casper by then. Influencing behaviour is just one illustration of the power that power players wield. But, to be honest, it's the intimidation and lack of control that makes you impotent. There are a lot of "If you do this... then" and "If you don't like it, we have someone else."

Professionalism comes first, and I made every effort to maintain that level of dedication. At times, that consistency can be suffocating. The only reason the audience learns about issues on set or "tantrums" by actors is because the pressures of life become too much to bear at some point. It is significantly worse for women than it is for men. When the media reports on an actor having a meltdown on set, they frequently blame it on someone else or claim that the situation justified the reaction. The reported list of male outbursts vastly outnumbers the list of female outbursts. Nonetheless, when an actress reacts negatively in any situation, she is frequently called a diva or unstable. The gender disparity existed long before I was born, and it persists despite efforts to correct it.

The unfairness extends far beyond media attention. There has always been an underlying pressure, particularly for female actors, to maintain their physical appearance-whether for a role, a contract, or simply vanity. As a young adolescent, I was lucky in that I never battled to maintain a healthy weight, but the pressure to be small was always present. Studios don't want people who are healthy and happy; they want people who are skinny and productive. I was persuaded to hire a trainer who did not teach me good weight management techniques. Others educated me about workouts and cleanses to help me stay skinny. I did a lot of cardio and cut back on calories-the normal program for individuals who don't know any better. There were times when I would basically starve myself. Everyone around me complimented on how good I looked at the 2007 Kids' Choice Awards. "Jamie Lynn, you've never looked better!" commented my crew as they observed my thin figure. They complimented me on my beauty and slimness. As I proceeded down the "orange" carpet, the accolades continued. People constantly mixed compliments on my beauty with remarks on my petite stature.

The value of looking nice and staying fit has been ingrained in me since I can remember. My parents were always vain, believing that we needed to look the part by having a healthy physique. Although I never struggled with my weight, I did have times of self-doubt like most ladies. But it was on the orange carpet, with all eyes on me, that I was confronted with my insecurities. The conflict between appreciating how I felt and worrying that I had always been too big was raging. Executives used phrases like "healthy lifestyle," which signified something very different in their world than it did in mine.

Puberty added to the stress I was under. The body undergoes numerous transformations during puberty. Hormones are released, and bones expand, resulting in changes both inside and outside the body. However, the studios still want you to look the same. There is a lot of pressure to change your appearance-to become more ideal, symmetrical, and gorgeous. I never had any operations or injectables during my teen years on Nickelodeon. I breastfed Maddie for months after she was born. She preferred nursing on the left side, and I ended up being lopsided, much to my dismay. My deformed breasts required a lift; a decision I made for myself. The doctor recommended a tiny implant to give me the symmetry I desired. I still don't like the outcome of the treatments, as well as what remains of my breast tissue after breastfeeding my daughters. I may have another surgery to address my issues at some point. I still have body issues, but the decision to correct or enhance oneself by any means is distinct from the temptation to undergo a total makeover to conform to someone else's ideas. Even when transformation occurs, it is nearly impossible to sustain. However, the demands of entertainment executives have made many young women, both in and out of the industry, vulnerable to a variety of physical and emotional illnesses. Judy Garland as Dorothy in The Wizard of Oz is still the best illustration of this. Her chest had swelled two full sizes by the time they were ready to film and had to be severely taped down. To stay young and thin, the studio ordered her to go through a variety of diets and medications. She suffered for many years after that. Audiences are persuaded to believe that a particular look or size can be readily maintained. When Renée Zellweger portrayed Judy Garland in the film Judy, the concept came full circle. She had to be sewed into most of her costumes because she had been on a tight diet for months. Many women in and out of the entertainment industry struggle with low self-esteem and unrealistic beauty standards.

The ability to control the aesthetic can impair a young woman's confidence, influencing career decisions and the selection of initiatives that will best serve their long-term ambitions. This has happened to me several times in my career. I've met excellent experts whose vision simply didn't mesh with the way I saw myself. Sometimes it's as simple as changing your outfit or changing the arrangement of a song. Because I didn't have an option, I spent years appeasing others and doing what was expected of me professionally. It took me years to reclaim my strength and the confidence to recognize that I was capable of charting my own path.

The weight of duty that comes with success and celebrity can be daunting. I felt pressure to keep a show at its peak of popularity in order to ensure that everyone had a job and was compensated. My own support crew has always been limited. However, the more the star shines, the larger the team backing their efforts. A large team carries the danger of hiring swindlers and opportunists. With so many people involved in day-to-day operations—image, economics, and care—it's difficult to know who to put your trust in. As my sister's career grew, professionals came and went in quick succession. Many people really cared for Britney's well-being and worked to defend her interests. But she also became a target for unsavoury and devious individuals. Britney's experiences with people who only wanted to use her eroded her capacity to trust others and left her vulnerable, in my opinion. In the midst of it all, she'd had her heart crushed several times and became a mother. Even while she maintained her famous pop-star status, the cracks from previous disappointments widened into fissures. Britney didn't seek assistance for the problems she was having, and it appeared that practically everyone on the team was more concerned with keeping the money pouring in than with providing her the help she needed.

I'm assuming that this was one of the factors that led to the conservatorship being founded in 2008. Lawyers and third-party businesses took advantage of Britney's fame at a time when she appeared to be dealing with some emotional troubles. My sister didn't appear to be in good health, and those closest to her at the time, particularly my parents, thought the conservatorship was the best way to safeguard her and the riches she had amassed over her career. I believe their sole purpose was to keep her safe at a time when she couldn't do it for herself. My father, Jamie, who was no stranger to adversity, collaborated with lawyers and the court to create a trust that would benefit Britney. In 2008, I was sixteen years old and about to give birth to my first child. I was aware that things were terrible for Britney, but I was preoccupied with my own life. I supported her during the moment by remaining loyal to her, listening to her, and defending her in any way I could. As a daughter, I behaved as any well-meaning person would. I recall what it was like to disagree with my parents. In this scenario, I was nothing more than a sister and a daughter.

Many people believe that my adolescent pregnancy ruined my job prospects. They couldn't be more mistaken. Maddie, I feel, saved me from years of possible unhappiness. My siblings had already shown me the darker side of celebrity by the time I was sixteen. There is a long list of young actresses and performers who have struggled with addiction, despair, and anxiety. I struggled with anxiety and didn't recognize how much it affected me throughout my childhood. I'm not a doctor, and I make no claims to knowledge beyond my own. Perhaps certain people are susceptible to emotional disorders brought on by Hollywood influences. Imposing unyielding demands on young performers who are going through difficult developmental stages may put them in jeopardy. I'm not sure. I believe that too much celebrity and riches, along with pressure, can lead to poor coping techniques that inflict permanent harm.

My pregnancy took me out of that world at a time when I was most vulnerable to negative exposure. I avoided the added stress of my partying companions and initiatives that didn't feel right for me. I was an emotional disaster in the summer of 2007. I felt helpless in the face of my career's velocity. Who knows what might have occurred if I had stayed in that situation? To be honest, the pressure and emotional volatility of adolescence made me vulnerable. Surprisingly, Maddie added a sense of steadiness. I was compelled to accept responsibility for both her and myself, which altered the course of my life and my concentration. Maddie had become my entire universe, and being her mother made all the difference.

10.

The Day My World Stopped

My life was irrevocably altered in February 2017 as a result of my daughter, Maddie's, accident. After church on a typical Sunday at the Hammond residence, we stopped by Jamie's parents' place. Maddie requested permission to ride an ATV and was involved in an accident. The catastrophe occurred while the girl was driving around a lake; the automobile tipped over, trapping Maddie underwater. We ran into the water to help the girl, who was in a state of panic and sorrow. The stressful rescue occurred as we attempted to lift the ATV to free Maddie. Maddie was eventually saved because of the tireless efforts and prompt arrival of rescue workers, but her health was critical.

Maddie went into a coma after being taken to the hospital. Doctors were unsure about her health, but my family continued to pray. Maddie's condition gradually improved while in the hospital, despite initial memory and behaviour issues. Maddie's recuperation took a long time, but she was eventually able to return home and continue her excellent recovery.

Maddie's injury caused me to rethink my life and values. I chose to become a Catholic, modify my lifestyle, and devote more time to my family. This experience further strengthened my belief in the power of prayer and miracles. Finally, our family gained a new addition, Ivey, who brought us all joy and strength.

11.

A Good Mom

Even before I considered becoming pregnant, I had clear views about how I wanted my children to be raised. My children would be stable and consistent. As I already stated, I wanted to protect them from the chaos that my parents' relationship caused for me and my brothers. I can't deny that if my attempts to start a family with Casper had been successful, I might have ended myself exactly where I started. Fortunately, I had learned enough in my youth to know that our disagreement would lead us down an undesirable path. I understood that going it alone with parenting was preferable to staying with him. For a time, I thought it would just be Maddie and me. So be it if I remained a single parent. But as the years passed, I began to consider what it might be like to welcome a man into my life. I knew they'd have to grasp the rules I'd adopted to regulate my existence. I refuse to fall victim to or expose my children to anyone who exhibits addicted and abusive habits similar to those displayed by Casper. I couldn't trust myself to spot warning indicators in the early days of my budding friendship with Jamie. There weren't any with Jamie, but I still didn't have the confidence to trust my gut impulses. It took time to reconnect with my intuitive voice, and with someone like Jamie, who has well-defined values for himself, it came easier than I imagined. Finding out what works in my own life is the flipside of lying. Momma told me a long time ago that once you lie, you have to tell a bunch of additional lies to cover the original one. Making good judgments in my life works in the same way. It became easier for me to continue making good choices after I made one. I discovered that balance, stability, and continuity are essential components of my well-being, and Jamie shared these principles with me. Our shared ideals became our foundation, and falling in love was a gradual process for both of us.

My background has taught me to regulate my life precisely and precisely. I'm a planner and a calendar keeper. I make colour-coded and alphabetized lists and charts. My job necessitates a lot of travel and time on set where I am unable to use my phone. No one is allowed to use a cell phone during production because producers are anxious that images, recordings, or information would be leaked and reveal plot twists or expose behind-the-scenes stuff. To make things easier for everyone, I created mini information notebooks that Jamie and the girls can refer to at any moment. We have a thorough weekly calendar for the entire family so that we know where everyone is at all times. I give pickup times as well as the identities of the carpool drivers. Phone contacts for professionals and friends are provided. There is a tiny book with drug and dosing information. Can you see how I tend to plan for every contingency? My husband would describe me as a functioning obsessive-compulsive. He is correct. After Maddie was born, I learned that stability and scheduling gave me peace of mind. I wanted to make sure she had everything she needed, but I also didn't want to forget anything.

Years later, with a husband and two daughters, I've had to broaden my horizons and devise efficient methods of staying organised. My creative mind enjoys putting together these scheduling tools for my family, and it makes life easier for everyone. It's the aftereffects of growing up in a chaotic family where schedules were frequently modified and stability came in spurts. The need to have control over my time and environment is critical to my well-being. The key words are "feel like," because life has shown me that we have very little control over anything. We have control over our ideas, behaviours, and reactions. Beyond that, everything is in God's hands.

I'm merely a control freak on the side. Spontaneity allows me to participate in whatever my daughters are doing. I try to remember to be appreciative and to enjoy the tiny things in life. My concept of a good mother is based on my personal experiences. I feel that everyone's idea of what it means to be a good mother differs based on how they were raised. I knew from the beginning that my children's needs would take precedence over the needs of everyone else in my life. I always wanted them to feel appreciated and wanted, but also secure in the knowledge that they were my top priority. It was especially crucial for Maddie because of her experiences with her father. Casper did his best to be Maddie's father, but as the years went, he faded more and more. He was helpful after her injury and during her recovery, but he eventually disappeared for extended periods of time.

Casper had relapsed into using by the time Maddie turned nine. Maddie began to discuss changing her surname to Watson. Her determination was borderline demanding. We emphasised that she didn't comprehend the lengthy adoption procedure and that changing her name meant giving up the name Aldridge for the rest of her life. She argued that she did understand and that it was vital to her that she share our name. Casper was no longer paying her visits, and as his run-ins with the law escalated, I realised something had to change. I thought for months about what was best for Maddie and everyone else, including Casper's parents. I greatly wanted Maddie to have a relationship with her biological grandparents, but the schism between father and daughter made it difficult. I discussed it extensively with Jamie, my parents, and even my priest. I wanted to do the right thing, but most importantly, Maddie's well-being had to come first. I told Jamie about my darkest worries, how I despised playing God and making such a significant decision that would affect Maddie for the rest of her life. Jamie had always been in favour of Casper remaining Maddie's father in name and deed, and she had watched as Casper gradually faded from her life.

As I have stated, Maddie and Jamie's connection is certainly unique. He has become a father figure to her in the years since he joined our duo, and their bond has only grown stronger. She respects him not only as my spouse, but also as a parent. For several years, he had taken on the burden of parenting, which can be challenging at times. I had a difficult time ceding responsibility for Maddie's care at the start of our marriage. I'd been her primary provider for so long that shifting that dynamic was difficult for me. Jamie gradually gained my trust and demonstrated his commitment to Maddie's well-being. That faith enabled me to share my burden and incorporate him into all aspects of her life. After considering all of the options, Jamie and I decided to pursue adoption.

We spoke with Casper several times, who initially felt as if we were removing him from her life. I eventually persuaded him that I was speaking on Maddie's behalf. She wanted to share our surname and feel closer to us. Casper finally relented after a few weeks. Casper felt, if not good, at least satisfied Maddie would be happier this way after her initial interviews with mediators. The process took months and corresponded with Ivey Joan's arrival. We urged Casper to stay in our life for the rest of our lives. Unfortunately, as the months passed, he found himself in legal difficulty again and again, and he vanished.

Ivey's arrival in the world was more normal than Maddie's. There was no press or media coverage. In the 10 years since my first child was born, social media had emerged, and that platform offered us power over what was made public. We had the ability to share whatever we felt comfortable sharing with the rest of the world. Nobody would have known or taken images before us. I could crop and improve the photos to highlight the aspects of the trip that felt appropriate to share. Nobody would twist or misrepresent what I said directly. Jamie and I arrived late at the hospital. Momma and Daddy stayed with Maddie in the evening, who had been granted special permission to stay up late and miss school due to the arrival of her baby sister. She couldn't stop herself from laying out a special set of "big sister scrubs" to wear the next day.

The nurse who was assigned to me was fantastic. She made everything go more smoothly. I felt absolutely relaxed, whilst Jamie's frantic motions and pain were amusing. He appears to be the one giving delivery. He was so calm and powerful during Maddie's hospitalisation that I had no idea he'd be nervous during my birth. Jamie despises seeing me or anyone he cares about suffer in any manner. Unfortunately, the birth process can be difficult for all men involved, especially when the epidural is delivered only after contractions begin. The morning went off without a hitch, and Momma appeared to be enjoying herself. Ivey arrived, fulfilling so many fantasies, while Jamie grabbed my hand and glanced at the opposite wall to try to keep standing. Maddie entered the room beaming with happiness. We were engulfed in love and awed by one another.

Being a mother of two happens in an instant. The transition occurs in real time, and it was simpler for me than the months of pregnancy that had devastated my body. During Ivey's pregnancy, I discovered something about myself that I hadn't had time to explore during Maddie's: I despised being pregnant. I'm eternally glad for a baby-especially a healthy one. But what about the real pregnancy? I'm still not sure why, but I developed a form of prenatal depression and spent months fatigued, listless, and in physical discomfort. Breathing difficulties make me unhappy and difficult to be around. Surprisingly, I experienced unprecedented happiness within hours of giving birth. The reduction of symptoms, together with the baby's safe birth, is enough to alleviate the problem—I'm sure there's a hormonal component as well.

As reality sank in and Jamie and I became parents to two daughters, adjusting to our new normal went better than I expected. Ivey approached breastfeeding as if it were a sport. My passion of bonding with my baby and providing sustenance in this unique way was reignited the second time around. She latched quickly and only quit when she began asking for my boob in full phrases.

Maddie and Ivey are around ten years apart, just like Britney and me. It's strange to watch them interact. I occasionally see them and am engrossed in my own memories. Maddie wanted to do everything for Ivey when she was first born. I had to explain that some things can only be done by a mother. Maddie had to adjust to sharing me with her sister in the months that followed. This was easier for me because I had lots of time with Ivey when Maddie was at school. But Maddie was having difficulty grasping this concept. "Maddie," I said. For a long time, you had me all to yourself. Ivey deserves some of my attention. Remember, none of my babies will ever have complete access to me." That appeared to calm her down, and we all ultimately adjusted to our new lives. Our family felt whole after the adoption and the arrival of Ivey, as if the parts of a puzzle had been put together. Don't get me wrong: there may be a few more parts added in the future, but for now, everything feels exactly right.

Being a good mom to me entails making difficult decisions and creating boundaries. Limits inform children that they are safe and cherished. I've learnt through experience and observation that children and teenagers will test boundaries and attempt to assert control before they are mature enough to understand the repercussions. It bears emphasising that I do not want my daughters to suffer as a result of my mistakes, but I also need to give them time to be children, vulnerable in a society that can be both permissive and punishing. I grew up too quickly, and I always encourage Maddie to slow down and appreciate her youth. Time flies by without us wishing it gone. As an adult, I can now see the truth for what it is. We only have moments, therefore making the most of them is a gift. That's why I aim to be spontaneous and keep my home life simple. Work is something I try to keep apart from my family time whenever possible. I'm not a fancy girl, that's for sure. I dress up for a living, but my favourite outfits are large T-shirts and comfy shorts. I prefer to wear slides and shoes. My face is usually makeup-free, and my hair is either tied up or hidden behind a cap. I'm uncomplicated. I believe part of the reason I don't fret over my looks on a daily basis is that I want my daughters to perceive me as Momma, not a character. I value my time and dislike wasting it by wearing makeup. Unless I'm dressing up with Ivey, which may happen at any time.

I am continually striving to be a good mother to Maddie and Ivey. It means I have to be present every day, even if it means using FaceTime or a phone call. Ivey is still so little that she needs time, just like any other toddler taking up the world and learning by doing. Maddie is approaching the age when she would be humiliated to read about herself in this book. But it doesn't stop me from being her softball parent, doing everything I can to see every single game-even if it's via the internet. I show up for her by being accessible whenever she requires it and encouraging her to feel at ease in her own skin. I always have her back and absolutely love her-not because of anything she does, but just because she is mine. Okay, and Jamie's.

Being a good parent is made possible by the appropriate partner. I've always thought I'm bad at relationships. The truth is that being a decent partner is impossible until you're in the appropriate relationship. I'll be the first to admit that I'm not flawless. In reality, I'm a terrible wife on some days. I try to be as caring and supportive as possible most of the time. And Jamie understands me. He understands my eccentricities and convictions and yet loves me. Our parenting approach is tough, loving, and humorous. Ivey is too little to remark, but Maddie would tell you that we can be demanding at times, but always with love and respect. We'd say the same thing about her, for the most part. Except when she's pushing her new adolescent boundaries!

I, like many mothers, require my own place. Because of who I am, there isn't a lot of downtime in my life. I need to have a sense of purpose in almost everything I do. However, I do have a few vices. I enjoy mindless reality television, such as The Real Housewives, after Jamie and the girls have gone to bed. Late at night, you can generally find me gaping, mouth agape, at something spoken by one of the spouses while folding a massive load of clothes. Remember the word "purpose"? I also enjoy reading scripts. I enjoy immersing myself in the universe that someone has created for the screen. When I don't have time to myself, I enjoy a fizzy bottle of Coca-Cola. But only a bit. I'm striving to be a good role model!

We stay strong as a family by showing up for each other every day, loving uncontrollably, and avoiding driving each other insane. At the heart of it, I strive to be a good mother. It's not something you can master. Sometimes I have a strategy, and other times I just close my eyes and jump. I've got a safe landing spot. Jamie is my steadfast Louisiana man, and together with our daughters, we've formed a lovely family.

12.

You Can Take the Girl Out of Louisiana

My feelings about the way I conduct my life today are the same as they were when I played Zoey. As a young performer, the girl who realised a dream and became a celebrity, I seized and used every chance that came my way. Teenage me imagined a career in performing and singing. When I closed my eyes and imagined my future, glimpses of the performer I wanted to be appeared. Realising any desire needs the willingness to suffer, learn, and endure difficult events that ultimately change a person in fundamental ways, or so I've been told. For me, the journey from child star to teen mom to adult performer and wife has brought me full circle to what really makes me happy.

I made a vow to myself early on: I will do everything in my ability to provide a stable and pleasant atmosphere for my family. My children's needs will always take precedence over my own until they are able to do it for themselves. Years before I became a mother, Daddy's long drinking and the awareness of the absolute anguish and shame I'd suffered as a child, combined with Momma's incessant need to convince the world that everything was OK, provided the fuel for that commitment to myself. Becoming Maddie's mother confirmed that truth. I had no idea anyone or anything could stop me from honouring my vow. If I'm anything, I'm strong and steadfast in my obligations to myself and others. So, how did I slip so far off course for a while?

The decision to have Maddie and to try to establish a life with Casper were both instinctive and sensible. My intuition has always been a major influence in my life. I never considered not having her after I found out I was pregnant. Everyone else had their doubts. She was a gift for me and my adolescent heart. In the beginning, I genuinely felt Casper and I would heal our wounds and start a family. Love, especially young love, is a powerful force that has blinded me to not only rationality but also my gut feelings. I was disgusted with myself after making the same mistake over and over again in Maddie's first few years by enabling Casper's antics, which were so similar to my father's. It took years for me to get over those feelings, which only cemented my desire to keep abusive conduct from impacting my children in the future.

The pledge to them begins with me. I learnt how to take care of myself. Workouts that were previously geared to keep me thin and strong, with lots of cardio, were replaced with a more dynamic approach to fitness that included both body and mind strength. Julie Day, my trainer-turned-friend, helped me to view food, my body, and my faith more holistically. This aided me in developing a healthy relationship with my own mind and body. But, like everyone else, when the alarm goes off in the morning, I lie there, staring up at the ceiling, and ponder, "What if I didn't go today?" Staying curled up in my bed is first appealing. Then I consider the consequences of failing to meet my own needs. My training program not only fortifies my physique, but it also helps me manage my anxieties and emotions. I've also resolved to talk about my worries and fears. It's my way of treatment. And I pray a lot. These habits are merely a small portion of how I keep this promise. The other component is more difficult. I had to relearn how to trust my own judgement. My relationship with Casper was plagued by the same codependent behaviours that my parents displayed as a result of my father's problems. Fear and negativity kept Casper in my life for far too long. For a while, my childhood traumas infiltrated my relationship, and I almost began to feel I was condemned to repeat my parents' mistakes. That was one aspect of my Louisiana existence I had no desire to keep.

My work and the resulting emotional trip, which carried me from Louisiana to California and beyond, led me back to my roots. The experiences that were so important in discovering what works for me confirmed how much I appreciate the simplicity and calm of a Louisiana existence.

I realised early in my career that I didn't want to live in Los Angeles. I was never a fan of the city's fast-paced energy. Don't get me wrong: I can keep up, but the vapidity of Hollywood never felt like home to me. I enjoy working there, and I admire the dedication that industry professionals put into all they do. It's incredible to see a project come together. A lot happens between the time a script is optioned and the time it appears on the screen. I'm energised by the process of developing characters and bringing stories to life.

Whether on the small screen or a large motion picture, in Hollywood or on location, I give my all to my work and immerse myself in the environment in which I'm working. I investigate each location and strive to make it my own while I'm there. I go for a run to get a feel for the landscape and to find areas I want to visit. Because I try to dress casually, I usually go unnoticed. I spend so much time with my daughters that I don't think about being noticed. I manage extended shoots by bringing my family as much as feasible. Our girls accompany me on trips or come to see me on weekends. I also make frequent vacations at home. Maddie has a busy schedule. I value her time and appreciate it when she can join me on location. Their help is crucial and keeps me grounded when I'm away from home. The ephemeral aspect of being an actor sometimes leaves me feeling untethered and unconnected. I've discovered that having the people I care about around me supports me and allows me to be a mother, wife, and performer.

My job allows me to have new experiences, such as playing roles and spending time in different places, but when I'm done, I return to Louisiana. Home is both the place I love and the people who surround me. It's when I abandon my persona, cast away my roles, and anchor myself in the security of the life I've created. When I return to Hammond, I cling to the comfort and predictability of the everyday. It's where I become Jamie Lynn, wife and mother. Both aspects of my life are equally tough, but my family keeps me tremendously humble and rooted in ways that performing cannot.

As an adult, I've discovered that my Louisiana ways, the things I enjoy most about life in the South, are within me. Momma and Daddy instilled in me a set of Southern ideals that have been ingrained in who I've become as an adult. The South offers me a sense of warmth that individuals from other sections of the country don't. It's not better or worse; it's just mine. I was raised to respect and defer to my elders-you gain respect by providing it. Manners are vital. Throughout my career, I tried everything in my power to maintain my moral compass. Despite my mistakes, I accepted responsibility for them all and sought to go forward. It's easy to veer off course in the entertainment industry, especially if you lose your ethics. The more popular you get, the easier it is to lose those aspects of yourself. For me, I do my best to maintain a strong moral code, accept faith, and surround myself with individuals who share my values. Living in Louisiana helps to reinforce these concepts for me.

Everyone takes a piece of their heritage with them. I absolutely do. The scope and size of the job I undertake vary. Even for something as simple as an interview, I am determined to present my thoughts and reactions in a way that captures the core of who I am. At this moment, I'm comfortable being myself, and I want that to show. It took me years and a few blunders to get to this point and regain my confidence. I've made mistakes and paid for them. Sometimes I'd start a project and realise it wasn't going to work out; I paid for those with more than money. Other times, someone else makes a mistake and pays for it. I've turned down a number of lucrative positions that may have advanced my career. I never do anything that doesn't feel right. Don't get me wrong: there are those meetings where I wonder if I truly want that particular job. But that's the beauty of the entertainment industry: you turn in expecting an offer for a role, and the meeting leads to a completely unexpected outcome and offer. Some CEOs who have seen my work mistakenly believe they know who I am. Their level of expectation shifts once we meet, and new opportunities present themselves. This was the situation when I discovered the Netflix show Sweet Magnolias. I was intrigued in working with a team on a music/film project called Roots when Ivey was born. Songwriting, which is basically storytelling placed to music, reminded me how much I enjoy being a part of the visual medium. I began to consider how I could combine the two. The music was finished, but I required a creative team to flesh out the notion I had in mind, which evolved out of the changes in my life since Maddie's injury. I travelled to Los Angeles to meet with Netflix and Hulu execs. I met with two Netflix execs who were kind and we talked about a variety of issues. And, just as in a movie, one of the women asked if I wanted to act again. "Yes," I answered. I'd love to. "I'm ready to get back to work," she said, explaining that a new show was about to begin production, and I would be great for one of the roles-but not the lead, and I'd have to audition. It was a terrific way to get back into a series. They sent me "sides" right away, and I adored the character. Within a day, I received a call informing me that the production crew was leaving for Atlanta the next day and that if I was truly interested, I needed to see them for breakfast that morning. "We still need you to read, Jamie Lynn. But we're feeling quite fine. Oh, and we start in Atlanta in three weeks. Will that work?" The timing and circumstances couldn't have been better. God was clearly pulling the strings.

One of the things that most people find surprising about me is the dichotomy of my personality. I can be quite serious, earnest, and introverted. On the other hand, I am direct, amusing, and engaging. I recently finished a photo session. If you've ever done a photo session, you'll know that the glitz that appears on the page takes hours to achieve. I don't always have the same team to help me improve my image, so I make it a point to put everyone at ease as soon as we arrive. The true geniuses are those who work behind the scenes in dress, cosmetics, and hair. Print shootings differ from film shoots. Photos necessitate a variety of poses that capture me as myself. I bring my personality and sense of humour to the process. To create an authentic image, I incorporate acting components into my print work.

When I'm familiar with a team, I feel at ease and can get started with the stylist. They are always well prepared, some better than others. We lay out a variety of clothing and accessories and bring the concepts together. A good stylist creates combinations; a great stylist knows who they are and delivers a vision. Sometimes numerous people weigh in on a look. But the final decision is always mine-remember the control thing? Don't let anyone convince you that cosmetics are merely a mask. A makeup artist is a true professional. To be honest, they are exceptional at maximising a person's assets by utilising shading and light. I especially appreciate working with a makeup artist who makes me look like a put-together version of me rather than a doll.

There is a whole different attitude to hair. The hair professionals collaborate to create a colour and hairdo vision. Each costume gets its own hair and makeup change. I usually like what they put together, but if I don't, they make changes. To be honest, I usually wait to see how things seem on camera or on a computer screen before interjecting.

While hair and makeup work together to alter me, I try to relax and frequently converse with the group. When I'm in the makeup chair, it's like sitting around with a bunch of folks, talking about everything from shoes to children to world events. I sat silently recently when the issue of young Hollywood came up and someone gave a name. They laughed when I inquired, "Who's that?""Someone said, "Come on, Jamie Lynn-you know who that is." I responded politely, saying that a full-time mom living in Louisiana has very little time for celebrity news. It reminds me how distinct the two portions of my life are and how much I value that arrangement.

Growing up as a dynamic performer and athlete, I became accustomed to shifting in front of people. It's a byproduct of the job. In a professional setting, I do what needs to be done since there is no time for inhibitions. To achieve a look, I must try on several sorts of garments and combinations. I'm aware that each image conveys a story or showcases a facet of my personality. I sometimes look in the mirror and despise what I'm wearing. But it's a look, and it helps me become the version of myself that we're all trying to capture on film.

In order to psychologically prepare for the day's filming, I established an internal dialogue. I may arrive on set feeling like my boobs are positioned incorrectly or that my legs need to be tanned more, but the shot must be completed—and that is my job. When I push the shutter, I take the role that is meant for a particular shot. It's acting using facial expressions and body language.

When a team prepares me for a role, it's a distinct appearance for a character I bring to life. The most unusual component of this for me is dying my hair an entirely different colour. I normally have to do this several weeks before a shoot, and staring at myself in the mirror can be disconcerting. The result can be diametrically opposed to what I would select for myself. But I remind myself that it's only temporary. The advantage of wearing a colour over time is that it makes it much easier to slide into character. For example, in a series shot, I'm frequently dressed similarly, and once the clothes and makeup are on, I can easily go into character. I find it motivating to play a character like Noreen on Sweet Magnolias. She is living a life that is very similar to mine. Infusing her with a strong spirit feels almost healing to me. She must take command of her life and prepare for a kid without the help of a husband or fiancé. Noreen and I have very similar life experiences. When I'm filming, I think to myself, Dang, she's got her crap far better together than I did.

My past penetrates every part of my acts. My upbringing has shaped my pursuit of perfection and commitment to professionalism. I practise my lines and fine-tune my performance as needed. Dedication to my art pervades everything I do in order to develop a reputation for dependability and competence. I want to leave the stage knowing that everyone regards me as a consummate professional. Within those boundaries, my integrity is paramount. I remain true to myself and the roles I play. To be authentic, I must feel at ease in whatever part I play. Because I enjoy inventing personalities, I can be at ease in a variety of situations. I can play an ingenue, even though that is not my personality, and I can also play an antagonist, especially one who is misunderstood. At heart, I'm a storyteller. The medium is unimportant. I want to be a part of a fantastic story with a character that has depth and purpose. The beauty of becoming a part of any story's journey is that it will eventually lead me back to the steadiness of living with my family in Louisiana.

Writing and performing music allows me to share aspects of myself and tell stories based on my experiences. It also allows me to use my imagination to create stories about life and love. Character development, storytelling, and performance are all aspects of being a songwriter and performer that appeal to me. By default, so much of who I am and where I come from is intertwined into almost every song I've written. When they learn how many songs I have in my catalogue, I believe almost everyone is taken aback. Only a few of the over a hundred songs I'm credited with have been released as of this writing. I've created chart-topping tunes for artists such as Jana Kramer and won awards for my work. When the time comes, I hope to work with other performers to bring more of my music to the public.

Timing has become an important component of my existence. I wear a number of hats and want to be totally present in that particular work. I wasted years doing what others believed was best rather than what I felt was best for me. For the time being, I'm enjoying being a mother, performing, and working with Jamie to attain our mutual goals. I'm proud of my roots and the life I've built in Louisiana with my family. I can't fathom living anyplace else, and sharing this part of myself with the world strengthens my connection to everything I adore. The road from teen mom to who I am today, with all of its ups and downs and self-discovery, has convinced me that I need to do something for myself, something that would benefit my entire family. I want to live a life that is full of generosity and genuineness.

13.

My Testimony

My sister broke her silence about the harsh nature of her conservatorship in 2008 on June 23, 2021. Throughout the weeks that followed, she had the opportunity to speak freel-to share her truth-on the globe stage of the media and the internet. During a handful of her speeches, she made broad accusations, referring to "my family" and "those who should have helped." My sister never revealed what or who was genuinely to blame for her difficulties. By ignoring this, she unleashed an assault of hatred on me and my family.

Her references to me made me dizzy. I've always had her back. I've been there for Britney since the beginning of her difficulties. I helped keep Britney's emotional outbursts secret from the world because I was too young to know better, to comprehend that it's acceptable if you're not okay. It started when I was in my teens, when I had to debunk rumours spread by my classmates, and I continued to protect her until recently, when she decided I didn't need guarding and threw me to the media wolves.

Despite her remarks, I continue to support what is best for her. I'm merely sorry that in her current state of mind, she can't assist me in the same way. My brothers and I have been traumatised by my parents' misguided sense of loyalty and success, the impact of exposure, and the negative side effects of celebrity. I'm not seeking sympathy. I want Britney and the rest of the world to know that she isn't the only one who bears the wounds of our early years of misbehaviour and manipulation.

I am eternally grateful for my job and the events that have brought me to this point in my life. But that was the result of good fortune, hard work, and owning up to my mistakes along the road. My sister's rant casts blame without any self-reflection.

Despite the developing instability in our home, I want to emphasise that my early childhood was enjoyable. However, we were not unlike many other families at the time. Everyone's attention, particularly my sister's, fueled my eventual need to gain her approval and acceptance. I'd do almost anything to stay in her good graces and had been manipulated my entire life. My parents coerced me to be a version of myself that supported the family-that is, my sister's ever-expanding career-which meant I was allowed to pursue my own aspirations as long as they aligned with hers. My goal was to be a decent girl, which left me exposed to my parents' schemes. Surprisingly, when I unexpectedly became pregnant at sixteen, I discovered the ability to think for myself and make decisions without needing their permission.

As a mother, I understand how much a youngster craves parental acceptance. As I previously stated, my sister was a mother figure to me, and maintaining our connection-knowing she loved me-motivated me to do whatever it took to make her happy. With the benefit of hindsight, I can concede that pacifying my sister, meeting her wants, and accommodating everyone along the road just added fuel to the fire. The fire has spread to become an inferno.

Early on, I was afraid that if I expressed my concern for her well-being, I might lose my sister's respect and love. Later, I was preoccupied with my own life, and my parents assured me that Britney was well. She clearly wasn't. Britney's impassioned words covered the wrongdoings of everyone involved, without any mention to herself, in recent years, and this past summer in particular, when my sister talked to the public about her sentiments regarding my parents' premeditated attempt to seek recognition.

Living through an unthinkable nightmare with Maddie over the last few years, I chose to make adjustments in my own life in order to avoid being dragged into the drama in which my family is so prominently involved. However, it has not been easy.

I was taught to be the most dedicated sister from the time I could follow orders. My parents were not required to inquire. Britney has always been a favourite of mine. It's usually the way things work. Devotion can take various forms, and mine is profound, abiding, and everlasting. Millions of kids my age were kneeling at Britney Spears' shrine when I was seven, learning what it meant to be faithful to my family. Britney's fan base grew dramatically while I was behaving, clearing a route, staying out of trouble, standing aside, and making sure I didn't upset my sister. No one was happier for her than I was. I knew how hard she worked for it and how much our family had given up to support not only her ambition, but mine as well. However, there were compromises, justifications, and possibly too much tolerance. Initially, I just thought, This is typical. It's how all families care for and protect one another. Growing up a Spears, on the other hand, has never been normal or ordinary. The world at large has always criticised and assessed us. That is where the problem resides. Nobody knows how calculated the press can be better than my sister. Everything she says is twisted and changed to serve a purpose. Words are important in our world and should be used with care.

If I'm guilty of anything, it's allowing the issue to persist by failing to speak up earlier in her career. I frequently wonder if it would have made a difference if I had. There are things I should have said to protect my family's reputation from gossip, and other things I should have spoken when I realised something was wrong. I'm only now realising how my family's mindset of making everything appear fine and tolerating Britney's conduct got us to this point.

As a child, I quickly noticed that my sister's work took precedence over everything else in my family's life. I was young and had no say in the issue. I enjoy my life now, but from the time I was seven until

I was well into my adolescence, I wanted Britney to leave the industry and we could just go back to Louisiana. For years, the demands of her profession and my parents' reliance on her made me feel, if not small, then insignificant. So much emphasis was placed on Britney, preserving their assets, that I was left to fend for myself at all times. That was the only way I could do it: strive in vain to be the loyal, loving, and devoted Spears family member. No one shielded me from the fallout of my older sister's difficulties, nor did they prepare me for the price of our silence. We were a close-knit family shattered by money, skewed truths, and unspoken emotional difficulties. It is, once again, acceptable not to be okay. Those auspicious words can be attributed to Piglet from Winnie-the-Pooh.

I finally got the wake-up call I needed to make a change. During quarantine, when we were all back together under one roof, I witnessed the same childhood relationship through adult eyes. Britney felt upset at something insignificant. She screamed at me and got up in my face as I was holding Ivey, who was only 22 months old at the time. Despite my best attempts, Britney persisted in her assault, and Maddie had to step in between us to defend her younger sister until my parents could ultimately convince Britney to back down. My friends and I were noticeably shaken. I made the decision right then and there—NO MORE! Momma pleaded with me not to irritate my sister. "I'm Jamie Lynn." Please don't bother upsetting your sister any longer; you know how she is. She can know when you're stressed." I stood there, mouth agape. I couldn't believe she was asking me to ignore my sentiments and those of my children in order to appease my sister once more. Experiencing this scenario as an adult and a mother was the impetus I needed to leave the situation. I wouldn't want my children to pretend everything was alright in order to comfort my parents or sister, and I wouldn't do it myself. Although the epidemic required that we stay together, I made certain that the girls and I were not caught up in that loop of conduct.

As Britney's sister and the daughter of Jamie and Lynne Spears, I didn't want to be a part of the legalities put in place to protect her. However, a few years into the evolving conservatorship, when Britney made her will, she wanted me to serve as trustee for her two children only if she was unable to do so herself. This was separate from her team's proposal that I reside in the conservatorship as a trustee over her children's trust. After several months of serious study, I decided to step down from that position, noting the possibility of a conflict arising from the developing concerns. My responsibility was to remain neutral and act as a sister and aunt. I have never served as my sister's personal representative or financial conservator in the conservatorship. In essence, I've never made decisions on behalf of my sister. I was raised to be committed, to defend my family, and to respect the privacy provided to all families. I was always available to assist with any difficulties she brought to my attention. And now, as a result of her testimony, that creed has bit me on the backside once more. To my peril and that of my spouse and two girls, I have stood by and defended my sister.

Since her testimony, I've been charged and convicted in public of everything from theft to negligence. Jamie, the girls, and I have all received threats. There are times when I feel unsafe. I had spent the most of my life trying to protect her even when it wasn't in my best interests, and I had thought that her remarks would make it clear that I had no involvement in any of her problems. I've always done my best to protect my sister, but now I have to prioritise the safety of my two girls.

Thousands of people have turned their admiration into judgments and bias based on snatches of insufficient information and supposition from the media. If you are a member of the Spears family, you are deemed repulsive and reprehensible in the eyes of the public. I am guilty of loving my entire family and wanting the best for everyone. I've always done so. But I've made my own family, and that always comes first. And Watson is our surname.

When the conservatorship was put in place in 2008, I was a seventeen-year-old female with a new baby. My entire attention was on my daughter Maddie. I simply knew my sister's behaviour had altered dramatically in the previous year from my point of view. Remembering that time in my life brings back the loneliness I felt because my sister was not there for me when I needed her the most. Perhaps I should have done more when I lived in California, but I was a youngster at the time. Britney was the grown-up, and she had assured me that she was alright. I enabled many of the activities that contributed to her downward spiral at the time by accepting her proclamation. The world saw she was in distress, and it looked that the conservatorship shielded her at a critical time.

And now what? Except for the fact that Britney is my sister, none of this has anything to do with me. Whether there is a conservatorship or not, I will continue to love and support her. Other than dealing with the shrapnel her explosive testimony hurled my way, I have no stake in this media circus, but that pales in contrast to the sorrow in my older daughter's eyes when she hears the murmurs among her peers. I am aware of the truth. "I know it's not your fault, and I'm sorry for being so angry at you," my sister said in a recent text. I need you more than you need me, even though I'm your big sister, and I always have." I hope she shares these remarks with the rest of the world one day. I have no influence over what the media says and cannot be held accountable for something over which I have no control.

It took me over two decades to figure out what healthy dedication and loyalty to family look like. I still believe that while dealing with personal concerns and trauma, our family, like every other family, should be given the same consideration. Nobody wants their difficulties to be published in the press, followed by discussion and judgments from their own relatives. It is incorrect to presume that

Britney's celebrity precludes her or her family's right to privacy. But none of us have had any privacy, and my parents' effort to protect Britney from embarrassment and public humiliation may have come at a hefty cost that wasn't in her best interests.

There are no sides here, and no one can win. I care about and support my sister. I believe that my sister and the medical specialists she chooses can work together to achieve the best possible outcome for her future. This ordeal may have been motivated by her music, her contributions to the industry, and the money, according to some. For me, this has always been about the girl who sacrificed so much to pursue her dream of singing in front of millions. On the other hand, everything Britney had given up along the way: her privacy, dignity, and overall health. When the cameras are turned off and everyone has gone on to the next headline, I will still be there for my sister, no matter what we say or do. I am really grateful for the many blessings in my life. The individuals who love and support me are everything. I've followed my intuition. Jamie and our girls will be my top priorities, just as I am theirs. We've worked hard to create our lives, and everything else, the turmoil that surrounds us, will eventually go away. My responsibility is to safeguard those I care about with honesty and zeal. Nothing else matters in my life if I don't have health and balance. Life is a series of lessons that push us to grow. My tested and reaffirmed faith assures that I defend my family, provide unconditional love, and impart the ideals I hold dear in order to live a moral and good life. I've learned not to enable, and no matter how much I want to, I can't help someone who doesn't want to be helped. Devotion and trust must be acquired and, ideally, reciprocated. I'm still learning as I go, and I'm sure there will be many more obstacles ahead of me. It all comes down to knowing myself and living authentically. I must acknowledge that in the past, a little more faith and a focus on our benefits may have made a difference. I'm sure it does now.

14.

Breaking the Cycle

When people first meet me professionally, they undoubtedly assume they already know my personality. I was instructed early in my career to be what was expected of me for a job. Much of my time in Nashville was spent in a cycle of being everything everyone expected me to be. But, near the end of that experience, I realised I could only work for myself. The standard of perfection I had set for myself was based on the vision of someone else. That didn't bring me any joy. Coming to terms with what truly gave me pleasure and how to nurture more joy in my life took place following Maddie's injury and my subsequent religious study.

Because of my upbringing, I learned early on the implications of making emotional decisions; making decisions based on how you feel about something will always bite you in the a$$. I recall so many times witnessing Daddy walk out the door because he believed he needed to-that he couldn't function without a drink. He lacked the sensitivity to evaluate how his actions affect everyone around him. I feel the same is true of Momma, who allowed actions that had serious consequences for the family and her children's well-being. My brother, Bryan, did the same thing frequently, whereas Britney struggled to make positive decisions that benefited herself or others. In the opposite direction, I spent years doing things that seemed both terrible for me and right for everyone else. It was nearly my undoing.

In the years since Maddie's miracle, I've had a spiritual awakening. I've changed my mindset on how I live and make decisions on a regular basis. My philosophy is founded on gratitude and a desire to give. I make an effort not to do one thing while feeling another. The word "authentic" is what helps me maintain my resolve. In other words, I must be honest to myself. I want to be the same person whether or not anyone is looking, which gives me internal accountability.

Life has bestowed upon me so many valuable blessings that my objective is to return them. I know that watching my child cease breathing and pass away altered me forever. I began by aggressively praying for those in need. I believe in the power of communal prayer to bring about peace. Giving power to something bigger than myself allows me to live in the now, which is different from how I used to approach things. If Maddie asked me to do something with her that I didn't want to do, I would frequently do it unwillingly, unable to share her excitement. I'd frequently grow annoyed with her or with myself. In any case, it served neither me nor her. I continue to do things I dislike. In truth, we spend the majority of our lives doing things we don't want to do. For me, the difference is that I reframed how I make promises. If Maddie asks me to do something I don't want to do, I think about how it will affect her. My heart isn't totally involved, but hers is, and when we're in it together, I share in her joy. Ivey consumes time like I've never seen before, and I'm a really impatient person. When I take her to the farmers market to pick out fruits and veggies, she always takes three times as long as everyone else. She is, after all, just three years old. I admit that there are occasions when I make a mistake and consider the things I could be doing. Until I see her expression. Her utter delight is contagious, and it reminds me why I took her to the market in the first place. I know I'll never regret spending time with my daughters, but I'll berate myself if I deny them playtime or a game of catch. I used to be brilliant at finding reasons not to do anything, but I made a conscious commitment to be as selfless as possible with my family and realise that giving my time reaps amazing rewards. There is no hiding from myself without justifications. My internal and exterior dialogues are more in sync, and I am living more truthfully.

Keep in mind that this is a process, and I am continually learning as I go. In the case of Ivey, I know that in the time it takes her to walk over to the market and look at two stalls, I could pick out the groceries, get home, cook, and serve a meal. The difference, however, is in abandoning control and being present in the moment with integrity. Committing takes some effort on my part as well. If Jamie wants to take me out on a date later in the week and I agree, I tell myself that all week. "I will go to dinner." Going out to supper isn't a chore in and of itself. However, after a long day of work, rehearsals, dance, and chores, it might be tough to generate the energy to go out. Speaking out loud holds me accountable.

Nothing makes me happier than seeing people I care about happy. It gives me hope in life and motivates me to give of myself even when I don't want to. We tell our children, like millions of other parents, that life is about doing things we don't want to do and, if we're lucky, getting exactly what we want once in a while. Jamie and I work hard to instil this idea in our daughters during their formative years.

My own upbringing gave me a totally different outlook. My parents raised me with the "Do as I say, not as I do" philosophy. Looking back, I think the lack of integrity in their acts is what irritates me the most. The value of hard work, dedication, and maintaining appearances kept any of us from speaking from our hearts and thoughts. We all went about our lives doing what we thought was proper and ignoring the habits and actions of others. There was a big contrast between what we thought was right and what we actually did. You don't know the difference as a child. I sensed something was wrong early on, but my inexperienced mind couldn't draw the link. But as I grew older and had my own children, I realised the inconsistency in that approach. It was suffocating, and it still causes friction in the Spears family.

The cycle concludes with me. I express myself freely, often to the disgust of others. When I'm sad or irritated about anything, I tackle it in the greatest way I know how. It's something I try to do with my family so that we don't harbour deep resentments and disappointments. I need to live my truth and speak it. It's another way I stay accountable. It has assisted me in beginning to heal from the difficulties and disappointments of my past.

My current self communicates with my parents in a way that benefits me. If I don't agree with anything, I don't keep quiet because they believe it's the correct thing to do. Silence contradicts true living. I evaluate why I feel the way I do and what fixing the problem will accomplish. Then I tell you. Speaking my truth can sometimes only benefit me. But, more often than not, I give my folks food for thought. Pretending everything is fine will never benefit anyone.

My approach to talking with Jamie and our daughters should allow them to speak openly about unresolved hurts and lingering resentments. I can only speak for myself and may offer a different viewpoint. Sometimes we are so caught up in the moment that we only perceive things one way. Nonetheless, there are occasions when we agree to disagree. That seems fairly typical of most families. I'm trying to be my best self through action and encouraging my own family to speak their truth.

It's difficult for me to open up about career concerns or family issues. There is a significant distinction between speaking on my own behalf and speaking on behalf of my family members. When it comes to issues involving my sister or family, I can only speak for myself. As a family member, I have access to experiences and information that allow me to perceive things from a different perspective than the wider public. It is not my story to tell, and I have no desire to alter media reports.

The media has generated millions of dollars by revealing much of my personal and family life. The world is well aware of the negative consequences of such intrusive scrutiny. I saw firsthand how damaging living life from the inside out can be to others around me. Existing in this manner compelled my family to portray ourselves to the world in a way that concealed our respective inner struggles. By doing so, I believe we preserved the public's impression of Britney's persona while doing little to safeguard her as a daughter and sister or us as a family. If I'm going to break the cycle, I have to embrace my truth about the part I played in my family's life and how I was pushed into doing things for her that made me uncomfortable. I am responsible for so many things, but I will never take responsibility for the difficulties my sister or family suffer, nor will I ever blame anybody else for my personal difficulties. My family is very important to me.

Since I was a child, my parents' need to maintain appearances for the sake of the business has been a powerful Spears incentive. I was taken into the fold, and while I was granted professional independence and opportunity, I was also expected to do whatever was necessary to support the Britney business machine. My years of sheltering her and being her devoted sister were in vain. The ambiguity of her conservatorship testimony and social media postings has left me wondering what all of this was for. I miss my sister, but I can't be held responsible for things I didn't do.

Many things will be heard around the world. Some of them may be true, while others may serve different objectives. I'm not going to say anything. I've always worked hard and made deliberate choices that have led me along my own path, both emotionally and professionally. We have troubles, as do many siblings. However, my relationship with Britney and our challenges have nothing to do with conservatorship, but rather with the boundaries I established to ensure the welfare of myself and my immediate family. Britney's account of how she was managed and treated does nothing to change the cycle. We must all manage our lives and struggles in the best way we see fit. I'm constantly striving to strike a balance between truth and wisdom.

My approach to living my best life keeps me grounded and allows others to see the real me. I am the mom that constantly attempts to prioritise her children's best interests. I am the wife who understands both the benefits and the difficulties of raising a family in these unusual times. Even in an age where everything you want or need to know is at your fingertips, the answers to fulfilment can still be found within. They certainly do for me. What I say and do keeps me true to myself. When I sit down to talk about a project or an opportunity, my confidence and intellect pervade every element of the conversation. Before making a decision that would affect both me and my family, I make certain that I have all of the facts and that I have communicated my demands. I surround myself with sharp thinkers who understand how the business works, where it's going, and how to get things done. As a teen performer, I just took whatever opportunities came my way. Instead of doing something solely for the sake of making money, I now examine who I am as a person and how a particular opportunity reflects the image of the woman I am today. Pursuing life truly entails accepting responsibility for both my triumphs and failures-the good and the ugly. I am confident in who I am and intend to continue learning as I go. And after years of feeling disconnected, this is exactly how I prefer it.

Printed in Great Britain
by Amazon